CHINESE CUISINE

RECIPES AND ANECDOTES FROM CHINESE GASTRONOMIC CULTURE

WRITTEN BY MARGOT ZHANG
ILLUSTRATED BY ZHAO EN YANG

FIREFLY BOOKS

CONTENTS

MAJOR THEMES

FESTIVALS AND TRADITIONS

PASTRIES AND DRINKS

* Have you eaten yet?

CHINESE CUISINE

In China, people often greet each other with the phrase
"Have you eaten yet?" — either on the street,
at work or at home.

This simple question shows how deeply rooted
food is in daily life.

Eating in China goes far beyond the core function of
getting nourishment. It's also a way to socialize, to
communicate with others and show love and respect.

A meal is, above all, a time to be together and to
reconnect. The simple act of serving a guest a piece of
meat or some vegetables is a sign of affection or care.

SEEKING HARMONY

When it comes to eating, whether it's a festive banquet or a simple meal at home, the aim is harmony and balance between the dishes' different flavors, textures and colors.

A festive meal at a restaurant often consists of a cold appetizer, then dishes stir fried in a wok or a steamed or simmered dish. If the dish has a soft texture, there will also be something crunchy for contrast; a dish without sauce is balanced by a dish with a sauce; and spicy dishes are balanced by refreshing foods with a delicate flavor.

This desire for harmony is always present when it's a simple meal at home. For a family of three, a daily meal often includes three dishes and a soup: a meat-based dish, two vegetable dishes or a vegetable dish plus a tofu- or egg-based dish, and a soup to finish off the meal.

Harmony is also reflected between people, foods and the weather. During a heatwave, people tend to eat more light and calming foods to soothe the body and regain inner tranquility. In winter, broths and infusions made of yang ingredients (p. 91) help to shake off the chill.

THE THREE MEALS IN CHINA

In China, dishes are all served at the same time, placed in the middle of the table, and shared among guests.

The day often begins with a nutritious **breakfast**. People eat mostly hot, salty foods, despite the influence of Western culture. The breakfast menu varies widely by region but can include fried doughnuts, soy milk, wonton soups, pancakes or noodles, and *baozi* (steamed buns). People may eat breakfast at home or, when they are in a hurry, in the street.

Fried doughnut with soy milk

Wontons

Sesame pancake

Baozi

Congee (rice porridge)

Cheung fun (steamed rice noodle rolls)

Lunch, which is eaten around noon, often includes a vegetable dish, a protein and a starch. At work, lunch boxes or meal trays are common. To eat lunch outdoors, people may choose a one-dish meal such as *jiaozi* (dumplings) or a large bowl of noodles.

Classic lunch box

Pork pancake

Steamed egg

Noodle bowl

Jiaozi (dumplings)

Plain rice

Blanched vegetables

According to tradition as well as Chinese medicine, it's better to eat lightly at **dinner**, with easy-to-digest foods. Today, not all Chinese people follow this approach. Given that people are at work and breakfast is often eaten away from home, dinner has become a time when they get together with family or friends around more or less hearty dishes. But since people eat relatively early in China (around 6:00 or 7:00 p.m.) and are in the habit of taking a walk after the meal, there is still time to digest before going to bed, even if dinner is a heavier meal.

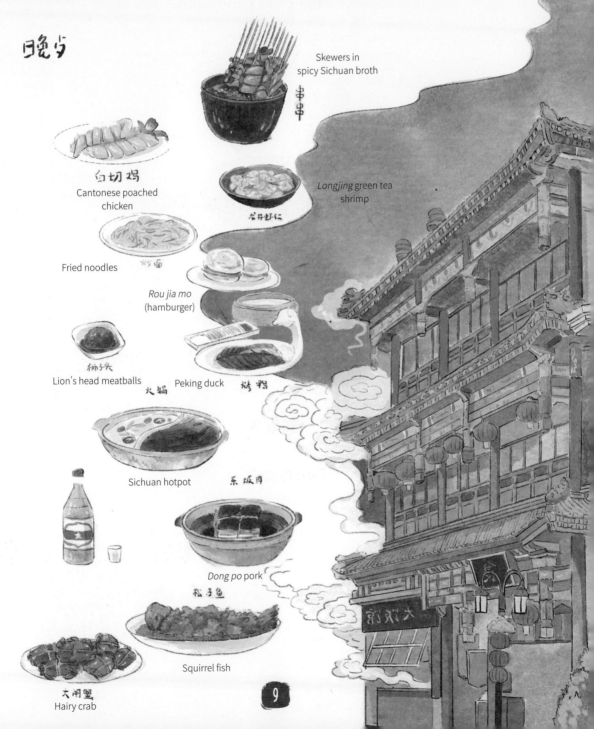

晚上

Skewers in spicy Sichuan broth

白切鸡
Cantonese poached chicken

Longjing green tea shrimp

Fried noodles

Rou jia mo (hamburger)

Lion's head meatballs

Peking duck 烤鸭

火锅

Sichuan hotpot

东坡肉

Dong po pork

松子鱼

Squirrel fish

大闸蟹
Hairy crab

BASIC UTENSILS

With a small number of cooking utensils,
you'll be better able to prepare Chinese dishes.

Wok: an essential tool for
cooking Chinese dishes

Chinese spatula: for wok dishes

Chopsticks

Chinese knives

Rolling pin: for making dumplings

Clay pot: for simmered dishes or
soups

Bamboo basket: for steaming

Steam rack (trivet): for steaming

Rice cooker

CHINESE KNIFE (CAIDAO)

A *caidao* is a large, multi-purpose Chinese cleaver: It can slice, score, chop, crush, scale, debone a chicken, tenderize meat and transfer ingredients from one place to another.

CRUSHED CUCUMBER SALAD

This is a very refreshing salad, ideal for a hot and humid summer day. Crushing the cucumber with the surface of the knife creates many microcracks in the cucumber, which allows the seasonings to really soak in.

SERVES 4

- ⅔ lb. (300 g) cucumber
- 2 cloves garlic
- Soy sauce, to taste (see p. 25)
- 1 fresh chili pepper, chopped (optional)
- A few sprigs of cilantro

1 Wash the cucumber well, then place it horizontally on a cutting board. Lay the flat surface of the knife over the cucumber and smash down lightly with your other hand to break the cucumber into pieces. Repeat with the rest of the cucumbers and the garlic cloves.

2 Put the cucumber, garlic, chili pepper and cilantro in a large bowl, mix with the soy sauce and chill for 1 hour before serving.

WOK

A wok is the most important utensil in Chinese cooking because it can do just about everything: sauté, fry, simmer, blanch, steam, smoke...

The traditional wok is a half-circle with a rounded base and is made of steel or cast iron. The carbon steel wok is used most often: it is not expensive and conducts heat very quickly.

The wok is heated to a very high temperature — 400°F (200°C) — to make certain stir fries. It is this intense heat that gives the ingredients a unique and indescribable flavor; this is called *guo qi*, "the breath of the wok."

HOW TO CHOOSE A WOK

The first thing to consider is the type of stove you have. Gas is ideal for a wok with a rounded base, but if you have an electric or induction stove, choose a wok with a flat base.

If you are new to Chinese cooking and want to make dishes that don't require cooking at high temperatures (like fried noodles or beef and vegetable stir fry), choose a wok with a non-stick coating.

The ideal choice is the carbon steel wok. Because it is light and heats quickly, it is an essential tool if you are a true fan of Chinese cuisine.

WATCH YOUR QUANTITIES!

Don't add too many ingredients to a stir fry, as it will lower the cooking temperature considerably and the ingredients will boil instead of fry. That is why a stir fry is always limited to two or three people. If there are more guests, increase the number of dishes rather than the quantity of a single dish.

SEASONING AND MAINTAINING A CARBON STEEL WOK

Traditionally, a bamboo brush is used to clean the wok, but you can also use a scrubbing sponge. Wash the wok with water and liquid dish soap, then rinse thoroughly. If your wok is rusty, use a scrubbing sponge to remove any residue.

Heat the wok on the stove on high until it smokes, add a thin coating of oil using paper towel and tongs, wait until the oil evaporates completely, and then add another thin coating of oil.

Repeat this process three to five times. Be careful not to burn yourself! After each use, wash the wok with water and liquid dish soap, towel-dry it thoroughly, place it over medium heat so it dries completely, and apply a thin coating of oil before putting the wok away.

BAMBOO BASKET

A bamboo basket is the best utensil for steaming thanks to its bamboo lid, which is not totally airtight and therefore does not accumulate condensation.

Also, because the baskets can be stacked, you can cook several dishes at the same time: not only dumplings, but also vegetables, rice, meat or fish, and even desserts!

Using a bamboo basket is very simple. Add water to a saucepan and bring it to a boil. Place the basket on top; be sure to use a basket that is the same diameter (or slightly larger) so it can rest on the edges of the saucepan and keep the steam in. If you have a wok, that's even better, because it can hold different sizes of basket thanks to its shape.

To cook dumplings or steamed buns, place parchment paper under each item so it doesn't stick to the bottom of the basket.

笼屉纸 Round paper liners
for steaming

CARING FOR A BAMBOO BASKET

After each use, wash the basket with water and liquid dish soap, rinse and let it dry completely before putting away.

TIPS FOR STEAMING WITHOUT A BAMBOO BASKET

If you have a wok but no basket, just put a steam rack (trivet) in the wok with a little water, then cover with a lid.

If you don't have a wok or a basket put a steam rack in a saucepan or pot.

Place the steam rack (trivet) on the bottom of the saucepan or pot. Add water (the water should not be higher than the top of the rack set a plate or bowl with the ingredients to be cooked on the rack, then cover the pot with a lid. If you can't find a trivet, use an empty can. You may have to think about how to deal with the condensation on the lid. Bamboo baskets are not airtight, so the lids don't accumulate condensation. This prevents water droplets from falling on the foods you're steaming. One solution for pots with lids is to wrap the lid with a dry tea towel so that the condensation falls on the tea towel instead of the food.

CUTTING TECHNIQUES

In Chinese cooking, cutting is a major part of preparing a dish.
A good cook is someone who has mastered knife skills.
Foods that are cut carefully and neatly allow for
uniform cooking while preserving the color,
texture and freshness of the ingredients.

滚刀

斜切

Cutting by rolling: Cut cylindrical vegetables (carrots, Chinese eggplant, cucumber and so on) diagonally, then roll them a quarter of a turn before cutting diagonally again. This technique gives pieces the maximum surface area to absorb spices and heat.

切菱形

Cutting into rectangles: Carrots and cucumbers are often cut in thin rectangular slices. First cut the vegetable into large pieces, then finely slice each piece.

Cutting diagonally: This technique is often used in cooking, especially for vegetables. It exposes more of the surface to the heat and allows vegetables to absorb seasonings more easily. Also, cutting diagonally protects the knife blade when vegetables are very fibrous.

Cutting cucumber in a spiral: Place a chopstick on each side of the cucumber lengthwise. Slice the cucumber on a diagonal without cutting all the way through. Turn the cucumber over, and this time cut it straight but still not cutting all the way through.

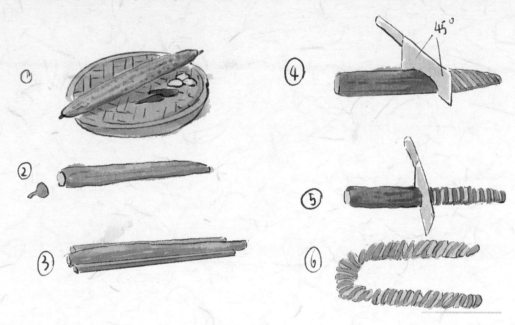

Cutting squid: For a nicer texture, prepare raw squid by making notches vertically, then horizontally, before blanching it in boiling water.

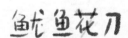

鱿鱼花刀

BASIC INGREDIENTS

Here are the basic ingredients you need to know
before getting into Chinese cooking.

FRUITS AND VEGETABLES

长茄

Chinese eggplant: has a thin skin and
very tender flesh. The skin is kept on
for cooking.

大白菜

Chinese cabbage (Napa cabbage):
one of the most commonly eaten
vegetables in China.

小白菜

Bok choy: ideal for quick cooking in a
wok with a little garlic.

空心菜

Water spinach: a very popular
vegetable in China. It is eaten sautéed
with a little garlic or hot pepper.

莲藕

Lotus root: with a crunchy texture, it
is used in salads and soups, steamed,
fried like a doughnut or eaten as a
dessert.

姜

Ginger: a core ingredient in Chinese
cooking and in traditional medicine.

葱

Green onion (scallion): an ingredient
that is used almost every day for
cooking.

蒜

Garlic: like green onion and ginger, it is
popular for making stir fries.

韭菜

Garlic chives: with a slightly garlicky
taste, they go well in omelets and with
shellfish or pork.

绿豆芽

笋

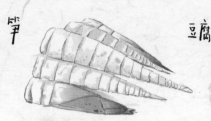

豆腐

Mung bean sprouts: often used in stir fried dishes or in soups.

Bamboo shoots: new shoots of bamboo that come up through the soil.

Tofu: made from curdled soy milk. Depending on the amount of water it contains, it can be called silken tofu or firm tofu.

木耳

香菇

红豆

Wood ear mushrooms: ideal for salads or soups.

Shiitake mushrooms: sold fresh or dried; if you're using dried mushrooms, soak them in water to rehydrate, ideally overnight in cold water, then cook.

Red beans (adzuki beans): a legume often used in desserts, either whole or pureed.

红枣

金桔

枸杞

Jujubes: used for sweet dishes and drinks but also as a spice in a broth.

Kumquats: called a "golden orange" in Chinese, this small citrus fruit is eaten fresh, in preserves or in jam.

Goji berries: are used in both Chinese cooking and traditional medicine; you can make a tisane by adding a few Goji berries, soaking them in wine or chewing them.

黑芝麻

花生

龙眼

Black sesame seeds: with a stronger taste than white sesame seeds, they are often used in baking.

Peanuts: their nickname in China is "longevity fruits."

Longan: often used in dried form to make sweet soups and infusions.

CONDIMENTS

生抽

老抽

Light soy sauce: a multipurpose sauce: it is saltier and thinner than dark soy sauce.

黑醋

Dark soy sauce: thicker and milder than light soy sauce. It has a longer fermentation period.

Black vinegar: the result of a long fermentation of sticky rice, it is fragrant and mild.

芝麻油

花雕酒

蛇油

Toasted sesame oil: used in small quantities after cooking.

Shaoxing wine: an essential product in Chinese cooking, it is a type of alcohol made from sticky rice, yeast and water.

Oyster sauce: used in Cantonese cooking to add flavor to dishes.

芝麻醤

豆瓣醤

豆豉

Sesame paste: used with soy sauce to make sesame sauce for seasoning noodles or salads.

Doubanjiang: a spicy sauce made from fermented soybeans and chili peppers, commonly used in Sichuan cuisine.

Fermented black beans: often used in preparing steamed fish or stir fries.

SPICES AND DRIED PRODUCTS

干辣椒

Dried chili peppers: found in southwest cuisine, they can be used whole or cut into small pieces.

花椒

Red Sichuan pepper

青花椒

Green Sichuan pepper

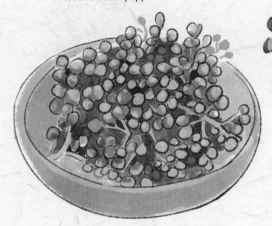

Sichuan pepper: it gives both a spicy sensation in the mouth and a tingling sensation on the tongue, with a lemony taste as the finish.

八角

桂皮

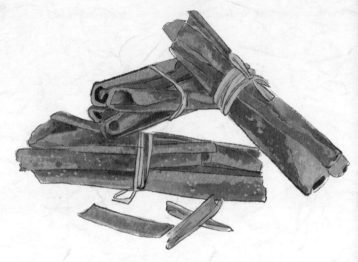

Star anise: only a little is needed to flavor a dish; it is one of the ingredients in five-spice powder.

Chinese cinnamon: it is darker than classic cinnamon, with a pronounced flavor: strong and slightly spicy.

陈皮

五香粉

Dried mandarin orange peel: the rind of the mandarin orange is dried, aged and fermented for years; it is often used in stewed meat dishes.

Five-spice powder: a ground mixture of star anise, Sichuan pepper, Chinese cinnamon, cloves and fennel seeds.

HOMEMADE OILS, SAUCES AND BROTHS

CHILI OIL

This very fragrant oil is perfect for adding some zip to your noodles or salads.

Preparation: 5 minutes
Cooking time: 20 minutes

MAKES ²/₃ CUP (160 ML)

- 3½ tbsp. (30 g) red chili powder
- 3 tsp. (8 g) raw white sesame seeds
- a pinch of salt
- ⅔ cup (160 ml) neutral oil for frying
- 1 piece dried mandarin orange peel
- 3 bay leaves
- 2 star anises
- 1 nutmeg
- 1 tsp. (5 g) Sichuan pepper
- 1 tbsp. (15 ml) black vinegar

180°C

200°C

1 In a container that is heat resistant to 350°F (180°C), combine the chili powder, sesame seeds and salt.

2 In a saucepan, heat the oil and all the other spices to 350°F (180°C), then remove the spices with a slotted spoon and continue heating to 400°F (200°C). Remove from heat and allow the oil temperature to drop to 347°F (175°C). Add the oil mixture in three pours to the container with the chili powder mixture. Add the black vinegar; the oil will start to bubble, which is normal. Let the oil cool, then decant without straining into a small jar and refrigerate. This oil will keep for at least 3 months.

SESAME SAUCE

To season cold noodle salads.

Preparation: 5 minutes

MAKES 4 SERVINGS

- 2 heaping tbsp. (30 ml) sesame paste
- 7 tbsp. (100 ml) cold water
- a pinch of salt
- 2 tsp. (10 ml) light soy sauce
- a pinch of superfine sugar

1 Place the sesame paste in a bowl.

2 Slowly add the water, stirring constantly (at first, the paste will be dense, but it will gradually thin out).

3 Add the salt, soy sauce and sugar. Mix well. Keep this sauce in the fridge for 2 or 3 days.

ALL-PURPOSE SOY SAUCE

A basic sauce for dumplings, salads, etc.

Preparation: 2 minutes

MAKES 4 SERVINGS

- 3 tbsp. (45 ml) light soy sauce
- 2 tbsp. (30 ml) water
- a few drops of sesame oil (optional)
- 3 tbsp. (45 ml) black vinegar
- a pinch of superfine sugar

1 In a bowl, combine the soy sauce with the other ingredients.

CHICKEN BROTH

Preparation: 15 minutes
Cooking time: 2 hours

MAKES 4 TO 6 CUPS (1 TO 1.5 L)

- 1 whole medium chicken, about 3 lb (1.4 kg)
- 8 cups (2 l) cold tap water
- 6 cups (1.5 l) spring water
- 3 green onions
- 1 star anise
- 3-in. piece ginger with peel
- 1 tsp. (5 g) Sichuan pepper
- 3½ tbsp. (50 ml) Shaoxing wine
- 1 tsp. (5 g) salt

1 Place the chicken in a large pot, add the tap water, turn on the heat to high and bring to a boil. Boil for 5 minutes, skimming the liquid regularly.

2 Remove the chicken from the pot. Throw out the cooking water and wash the pot to remove any impurities.

3 Fill the pot with spring water and heat on high. When the water is hot, add the chicken and all the other ingredients except the salt. Bring to a boil, then reduce heat. Simmer for 1.5 to 2 hours over low heat.

4 30 minutes before the end of the cooking time, add the salt, stir and continue cooking. Let the broth cool a little, then strain it with a sieve.

5 With the meat, you can make a small salad with warm chicken and a little soy sauce, a few drops of sesame oil, minced green onion and chopped ginger.

TRADITIONAL MARKETS

Visiting a traditional market is an excellent way to discover the local food culture.

Even though supermarkets have become increasingly popular in China, the traditional market is unique. It represents a city's identity: regional and seasonal products, the various personalities of the vendors, conversations in dialect, the crowd, bulk items in the stalls and street vendors offering all kinds of snacks that vary from one region to the next. For example, you'll find savory crepes in Shandong, crepes in Tianjin, skewers in Xinjiang, and countless types of cakes or sweets depending on the region.

富贵墟

RESTAURANTS

Restaurants in China are always specialized, such as by region or type of food (noodles, dumplings, hotpot, dim sum and so on). There are three types of restaurants: low-cost eateries where you can eat quickly and cheaply; small canteens, where local people stop by at mealtimes; and finer restaurants where you go with family or friends to celebrate (birthdays, weddings, births and so forth).

Noodle house

Dumpling restaurant

Tea house

Canteen with Sichuan dishes

In low-cost eateries and small canteens, people sit inside or on the outdoor patio. There are no servers (or very few), so you pick up your order yourself and pay at the cashier. There's a spot where you can help yourself to cutlery, sauces and paper napkins.

Fine-dining restaurants are often categorized by the type of regional cuisine or the type of dishes served.

A Peking duck restaurant

A Cantonese dim sum restaurant

A Sichuan restaurant

CHOPSTICKS AND TABLE MANNERS

The use of chopsticks is one of China's distinct culinary customs.

According to a legend, Yu the Great, founder of the Xia dynasty (around 2000 BCE), invented chopsticks by pulling two branches off a tree so he could eat a burning hot dish without having to wait. But no one knows exactly who invented chopsticks or when. Chinese chopsticks have a square section at one end and are increasingly rounded toward the other end. They are longer than Japanese or Korean chopsticks. They are often made of wood or bamboo. Some aristocrats in ancient times used chopsticks made of ivory, jade or silver.

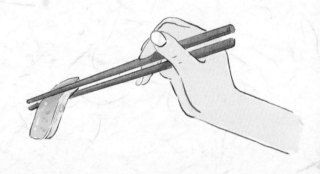

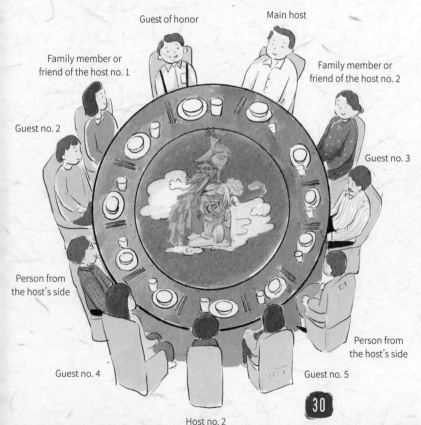

Guest of honor

Main host

Family member or friend of the host no. 1

Family member or friend of the host no. 2

Guest no. 2

Guest no. 3

Person from the host's side

Person from the host's side

Guest no. 4

Guest no. 5

Host no. 2

For an important meal at a restaurant, the main host and the guest of honor are always seated facing the entrance to the room.

The host always orders to avoid embarrassing the guests, who may not be familiar with the restaurant's specialties and might order inappropriate dishes or dishes that are too expensive and that the host cannot pay for. Of course, to show respect to the guests, the host always asks in advance which dish they would like, and out of courtesy, the guests always say, "I will have whatever you choose."

GOOD TABLE MANNERS

You must wait until the host picks up their chopsticks before picking up yours. It is frowned upon to start serving yourself before the other guests have picked up their chopsticks.

When you eat in a fine-dining restaurant, personal chopsticks are set to the right of the rice bowl or plate, on a chopstick rest, and chopsticks for serving dishes are placed to the right of the personal chopsticks. When you have finished eating, place the chopsticks in front of you horizontally.

Eat your bowl of rice holding it in your hand, with your chopsticks (in the other hand).

WHAT NOT TO DO

Stick your chopsticks in the bowl of rice.

Lick or suck your chopsticks.

Sneeze or blow your nose at the table.

Cross your chopsticks.

Speak to other guests while holding your chopsticks.

REGIONAL CUISINES

China, with its large surface area, is home to a number of very different landscapes: fertile plains, mountains, deserts, winding rivers and a very long coastline. The climate varies from subarctic to subtropical. Thanks to these contrasts, the produce and foods are very rich and diverse. The cuisine of each region is unique, influenced by its own terroir, customs and traditions.

THE GREAT CHINESE CUISINES

XINJIANG

Big plate chicken

烤全羊

Roast lamb

Nang (Uyghur flatbread)

TIBET

糌粑

Barley flour cake with butter

Yak butter tea

酥油茶

GANSU

兰州拉面

Lanzhou hand-pulled noodles

SHAANXI

Shaanxi *rou jia mo* (hamburger)

Lamb soup with crumbled bread

Kung pao chicken

小菜

Mapo tofu (p. 77)

Sichuan boiled fish

Pork belly with garlic sauce

Crossing the bridge noodles

SICHUAN

YUNNAN

Dai-style rice (accompanied by other dishes)

东北乱炖

DONGBEI

Dongbei stew

小鸡炖蘑菇

Mongolian hotpot

Chicken with mushrooms

京菜 **PEKING (BEIJING)**

Peking duck (p. 68)

SHANXI

Braised intestines

Braised shrimp

Tsingtao beer

鲁菜 **SHANDONG**

Baiju (sorghum alcohol)

晋菜

Sea cucumber

Shandong mackerel

ANHUI

徽菜

Pork with bamboo shoots

Yangzhou fried rice (p.64)

Chongqing hotpot

Lion's head meatballs (p. 71)

Squirrel fish

Fermented fish

Sweet and sour pork ribs

Hairy crab (p. 75)

苏菜 **JIANGSU**

Shaoxing wine

Ningbo *tang yuan* (p. 104)

Longjing green tea shrimp

浙菜 **ZHEJIANG**

Hong shao pork (p. 70)

湘菜

West Lake fish

Jinhua ham

重庆火锅

HUNAN

Buddha jumps over the wall stew

Yunnan wild mushrooms

Fish head with fermented chili peppers

闽菜

Dim sum

Cantonese roast duck

FUJIAN

桂林米粉

Guilin rice noodles

Soy sauce chicken

GUANGXI

Cheung fun (steamed rice noodle roll)

粤菜

GUANGDONG

35

THE 8 GREAT CHINESE CUISINES

SICHUAN CUISINE 川菜

Located in southwestern China, Sichuan means "four rivers." The geographical conditions have made Sichuan cuisine rich and complex in terms of flavors.

There are said to be seven flavors/sensations in Sichuan cooking: salty, sweet, bitter, acidic, hot (chilies), tingly (Sichuan pepper) and spicy (garlic, ginger and other spices).

In Sichuan cuisine, people like mixing different flavors to create several styles of complex flavors. There's *mala* sauce, which is a mixture of Sichuan pepper and dried chilies. There's also *yu xiang* sauce, which is a mix of fermented chili peppers, vinegar, sugar and soy sauce. *Guaiwei* sauce has an unusual taste and is a blend of sweet, acidic, salty, spicy, tingly and umami all at once. It's often in the form of a sauce for cold dishes.

GUANGDONG (CANTONESE) CUISINE 粤菜

Guangdong cuisine is without a doubt the Chinese cuisine that is best known around the world. Its richness is revealed in an extremely wide range of ingredients, its many preparation techniques, its ways of cooking and so on. Popular dishes are as plentiful as gourmet dishes.

Little known outside the country, the soups and broths are in a way the heart and soul of Cantonese cuisine. People enjoy soups not only for the taste but also for their health benefits (*yang sheng*, see p. 88). Ingredients are chosen according to the seasons and a person's state of health. Congee (rice porridge, see p. 63) is another specialty of Guangdong cuisine. It tends to be savory, using different ingredients such as seafood, meat and eggs.

SHANDONG CUISINE 鲁菜

Located in eastern China, southeast of Beijing, Shandong is a region that is rich in seafood products, grains and vegetables. The city of Qingdao, a former German concession, is known for Tsingtao beer, which is sold around the world. Shandong cuisine has greatly influenced cooking in the north. Some well-known dishes are mackerel dumplings four-happiness meatballs and braised shrimp.

ZHEJIANG CUISINE 浙菜

As a former economic and literary hub, Zhejiang is a region with good food and good wines: Shaoxing wine and Jinhua ham come from this region, as do Ningbo *tang yuan* (see p. 104) and fish with West Lake vinegar.

JIANGSU CUISINE 苏菜

Situated where the Yangtze River and the Grand Canal cross, Jiangsu is a region irrigated by lakes and streams. It is known as "the land of fish and rice." Freshness is one of the features of this cuisine. Well-known dishes include lion's head meatballs (see p. 71), Yangzhou fried rice (see p. 64) and Wuxi spareribs.

FUJIAN CUISINE 闽菜

Fujian cuisine is refined and light, with a penchant for dishes with sauce and for soups, such as the famous *fo tiao qiang*, meaning "Buddha jumps over the wall," made of quality ingredients such as shark fin, mushrooms and ham, simmered for five to six hours. The use of *hong zao* (the dregs of red rice wine) as a condiment is another unique feature of this region.

HUNAN CUISINE 湘菜

Bordered by mountains on three sides, Hunan has hot and humid summers. Here, people like spicy and tart foods. Fermented vegetables and meats are also very popular. Fermented red chili pepper is a specialty of this region.

ANHUI CUISINE 徽菜

Anhui is a continental region with open green spaces, rugged forests and mountains. Mushrooms and bamboo shoots are abundant, as are game and freshwater fish.

Peking duck served with thin pancakes, cucumber slices and green onions. The duck is rolled in the pancake and eaten.

Mongolian hotpot, or Peking hotpot, served with fine slices of mutton and sesame sauce. It is often accompanied by pancakes made of wheat, sesame and spices.

PEKING CUISINE

Beijing (formerly called Peking), the capital of China for centuries, is a city with a blend of several different cultures. Its current cuisine is a combination of four cuisines: halal cuisine, imperial cuisine, aristocrat cuisine and Shandong cuisine. These are some well-known dishes: Peking duck (imperial cuisine), Mongolian hotpot (Mongolian cuisine) and the famous Beijing *xiaochi*, which are small sweet or salty dishes that are eaten as a snack (halal cuisine and imperial cuisine).

Zha jiang noodles, made of fermented soybean paste.

SOUTHWEST CUISINE (YUNNAN, GUIZHOU, GUANGXI)

As the region that is home to the largest number of different ethnic cultures, southwest cuisine is so varied that it's impossible to generalize. In Yunnan, there are more than 200 types of wild mushrooms; in Guangxi, rice noodles are essential to daily life; and in Guizhou, fermentation plays an important role in the cuisine.

Guilin rice noodles, with slices of pork belly, fermented vegetables and chili peppers.

Maotai alcohol (a style of *baijiu*) made from fermented sorghum.

Yunnan hotpot with wild mushrooms.

NORTHWEST CUISINE (SHAANXI, NINGXIA, GANSU, XINJIANG)

In northwest *bai ji mo* cuisine, especially that of Shaanxi, the use of wheat and other grains is very common. People like the flavors brought out by spices and peppers. This cuisine is known for its wheat products: crumbled bread in lamb soup, bread stuffed with meat, noodles and *nang*, a round Uyghur bread baked in a traditional oven.

Lamb soup with *bai ji mo* (Shaanxi flat bread) that is torn by hand.

Nang, a round Uyghur bread baked in a traditional Xinjiang oven, with mutton skewers.

CHINESE AGRICULTURE

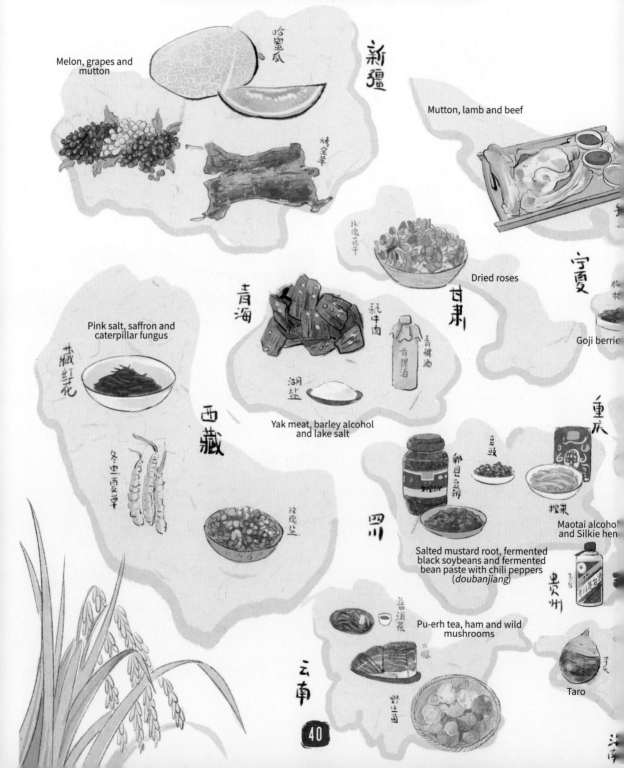

Melon, grapes and mutton

哈密瓜

新疆

Mutton, lamb and beef

烤全羊

玫瑰花干

宁夏

Dried roses

甘肃

枸杞

青海

Goji berries

耗牛肉

Pink salt, saffron and caterpillar fungus

藏红花

青稞酒

湖盐

西藏

重庆

Yak meat, barley alcohol and lake salt

冬虫夏草

玫瑰盐

郫县豆瓣

榨菜

四川

Maotai alcohol and Silkie hen

Salted mustard root, fermented black soybeans and fermented bean paste with chili peppers (*doubanjiang*)

贵州

普洱茶

火腿

Pu-erh tea, ham and wild mushrooms

Taro

云南

野生菌

40

For 5,000 years, rice has dominated China's agricultural activity and is the staple food of its people. Rice farming is spread over around 25 percent of the country's cultivated lands, mainly in regions around the Yangtze, the Pearl River Delta and in the southwest. The cultivation of wheat, like that of rice, is concentrated in the eastern part of the country, which is the most fertile.

内蒙古

Ginseng and pine nuts

人参

松子

东北

Dried beef

牛肉干

东北大米

Rice and wheat

北京

天津

河北

山西

陈醋

Sorghum vinegar and chestnuts

薛

苹果

小米

山东

大白菜

鸭梨

河南

洛阳牡丹

Cabbage and millet

Garlic

湖北

Peonies

Hairy crab

江苏

太湖蟹

Huangshan mao feng green tea

黄山毛峰

连藕

镇江香醋

Lotus root

野韭菜

安徽

祁门红茶

Black vinegar

Wild chives

Red tea

浙江

Agriculture in China is a major economic sector, with a rural population of more than 500 million people. China is the world's largest producer of wheat, rice, potatoes and many fruits and vegetables (eggplant, cabbage, tomatoes, apples, pears, mandarins and so on).

湖南

木耳

脐橙

江西

Kiwis and oranges

猕猴桃

Longjing tea and silk

龙井茶

nanthus owers

腊肉

Dried meat

广西

陈皮

广式腊肠

福建

岩茶

正山小种茶

台湾

Rock tea

凤凰单枞

广东

Pineapples and other tropical fruits

Oolong tea, dried sausages and dried mandarin orange peel

41

JIEQI: THE 24 SOLAR TERMS

 SPRING

People eat *chun bing* (wheat pancakes) to mark the start of spring.

The spring *jieqi* are:

Lichun
Start of spring

Yushui
Rainwater

Jingzhe
Awakening of insects

Chunfen
Vernal equinox

Qingming
Clear and bright

Guyu
Grain rain

In ancient times, Chinese people divided the annual movement of the sun into 24 periods, called *jieqi*, to mark changes in time. This was the result of a long process, generation after generation, of observing nature as it related to agricultural work. The name of each period evokes changes in nature and in farming activities at that time. In 2016, the 24 *jieqi* were added to UNESCO's Representative List of the Intangible Cultural Heritage of Humanity.

夏 SUMMER

Rice has five colors for the start of summer.

The summer *jieqi* are:

Lixia
Start of summer

Xiaoman
Small, full grain of wheat

Mangzhong
Formation of ears of wheat and rice

Xiazhi
Summer solstice

Xiaoshu
Minor heat

Dashu
Major heat

秋 AUTUMN

Steamed sweet potatoes and taro accompanied by tea.

Persimmons.

The autumn *jieqi* are:

Liqiu
Start of autum

立秋

Chushu
End of major h

火暑

Bailu
White dew

白露

Qiufen
Autumn equin

秋分

Hanlu
Cold dew

寒露

Shuangjian
Frost descen
(temperatures
and frost begi

霜降

Major cleaning for the arrival of the new year.

Tang yuan (glutinous rice balls in broth or syrup) for the winter solstice.

冬 WINTER

The winter *jieqi* are:

Lidong
Start of winter

立冬

Xiaoxue
Minor snow

小雪

Daxue
Major snow

大雪

Dongzhi
Winter solstice

冬至

Xiaohan
Minor cold

小寒

Dahan
Major cold

大寒

STAPLE FOODS

In Chinese cuisine, we distinguish between *zhu shi*, staple
foods made from starches, and *cai*, dishes made from
meat, vegetables, eggs or tofu. *Zhu shi* are essential in
the lives of Chinese people. They are so important
that a common expression, "losing your rice bowl,"
means becoming unemployed.

WONTONS

Wontons are small dumplings that are always served in soup or broth.
Their shapes and fillings vary by region.

广式云吞

Cantonese wontons with noodles in broth

四川抄手

Sichuan wontons with spicy oil

上海菜肉馄饨

Shanghai wontons with pork
and vegetables

福建扁食

Fujian wontons in a half-moon shape

北方馄饨

Northern wontons with seaweed soup
and dried shrimp.

Wonton filling is generally made with ground
pork, to which shrimp and/or different vegetables are added.

WONTONS WITH PORK AND SHRIMP

MAKES 20 WONTONS
- 20 wonton wrappers

For the stuffing
- 1-in. piece ginger
- 1 green onion
- ¼ lb. (100 g) raw shrimp, shelled
- ¼ lb. (100 g) ground pork
- 1 tbsp. (15 ml) Shaoxing wine
- 1 tbsp. (15 ml) light soy sauce
- 1 tbsp. (15 ml) vegetable oil
- 1 tsp. (5 ml) sesame oil
- ½ tsp. (1 g) ground pepper

For each soup
- 1 sheet dried seaweed, cut in strips
- 1 tsp. chopped green onion
- ⅔ cup (160 ml) boiling water or hot chicken broth
- 1 tsp. (5 ml) light soy sauce
- 1 tsp. (5 ml) sesame oil

1 Finely chop the ginger, mince the green onion and cut the shrimp into ½-in. (1-cm) pieces.

2 Place the ground pork in a large bowl, then add the wine. Quickly stir the wine into the meat by hand, always stirring in the same direction. Pour the soy sauce over the meat and stir for 1 minute. Add the shrimp, oils, pepper, ginger and green onion. Stir.

3 Take a wonton wrapper and moisten the edge with water. Place 1 teaspoon of stuffing in the middle of the wrapper. Fold the wrapper diagonally a bit off center, then fold from right to left and pinch with one hand between your index finger and thumb to make a pouch. Pinch again with a little more pressure so the edge is tightly sealed. Shown below are different ways you can fold wontons.

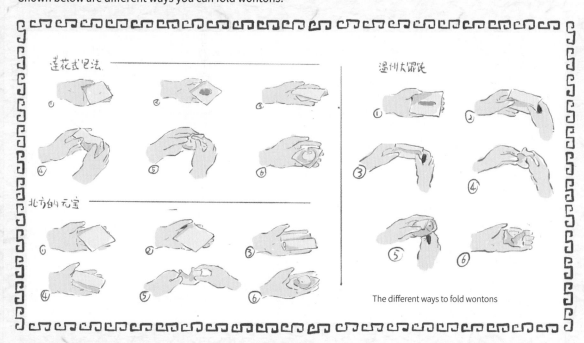

莲花式包法

温州大馄饨

北方的元宝

The different ways to fold wontons

4 Cook the wontons in boiling water. Once they bob to the surface, they are cooked. Use a slotted spoon to remove them.

5 In each soup bowl, place all the dry ingredients for the soup and add the wontons. Add the soy sauce and sesame oil to the boiling water or hot chicken broth and pour over the wontons.

NOODLES

In China, when people talk about *mian*, noodles, they mean the ones made of wheat flour. The symbol for wheat appears in the ancient Chinese character for *mian* — 麵.

There is an incredible diversity of noodles in China. The shapes, toppings and broths vary from region to region. Noodle lovers have a clear preference for fresh noodles; they are easily found at traditional markets or in supermarkets. Dried noodles, in packages, are mainly used in a pinch, when people don't have time to go grocery shopping.

> In China, noodles are not routinely rinsed after cooking. Sometimes noodles are kept hot and lightly covered in cooking water. This helps the sauce adhere better to the noodles.

拉面

Hand-pulled noodles: made from dough that is kneaded and left to rise several times. The dough is pulled and stretched repeatedly to get noodles of different widths.

竹升面

Egg noodles: these are a specialty of Cantonese cuisine. The dough is made from wheat flour and eggs. Traditionally, the dough is kneaded with a long bamboo pole, using all your weight to flatten it.

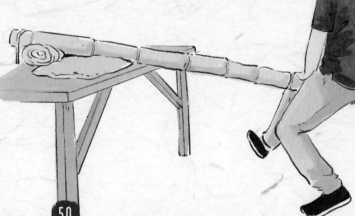

Knife-cut noodles (*dao xiao mian*): with a special knife made for this type of noodle, a block of kneaded dough is shredded to get strips of various lengths and then cooked immediately. This is a Shanxi specialty.

长寿面

面面

Longevity noodles: also called *suo mian*, these are very long, thin noodles, often sold in dried form. They are eaten in a broth or with a sauce. This is the essential dish for a birthday dinner because they symbolize long life.

Biang biang **noodles:** the dough is made of wheat. First, small oval pancake shapes are made, then marked with a straight line using a chopstick. The two ends of the dough are stretched to get a very long band, then the band is torn in two with both hands, following the straight line made with the chopstick.

Hanging noodles: this is a special technique for making dried noodles in China. After fresh noodles are made, they are hung on drying rods and left to dry naturally in the sun.

Knife-cut noodles: this is a fun way to make fresh noodles as a family; the kneaded dough is rolled out to make a thin pancake, then rolled up and cut in strips in the desired widths.

Scissor-cut noodles: a fun way to make noodles. Use a pair of scissors to cut the kneaded dough into small oval pieces.

In China, great importance is placed on the texture of the dough. The preparation and cooking are therefore crucial to get the texture, *jindao* or *tanya*, which can be translated as "bouncing on the teeth." This is different from the concept of al dente, which is more about the degree of cooking.

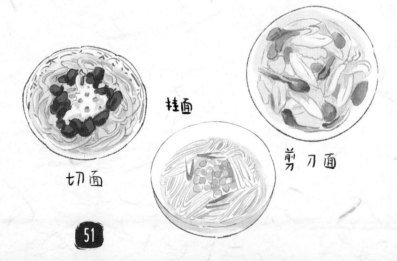

挂面

切面

剪刀面

BIANG BIANG NOODLES

Preparation: 1 to 1.5 hours
Cooking time: 2 to 3 minutes

MAKES 2 SERVINGS

- 1½ cups + 2 tbsp. (200 g) all-purpose flour
- 1 pinch of salt
- 6 tbsp. (100 ml) water

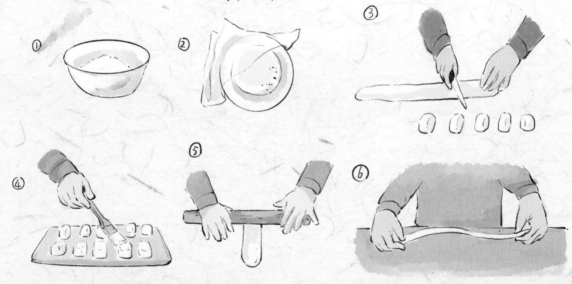

1 Combine the flour and salt, then gradually add the water while mixing well using a pair of chopsticks or a fork. The dough will not be smooth at this stage, which is normal – it should form lumps. With your hand, gather the lumps together. Knead until the dough is a smooth texture. Place in a large bowl and cover with a damp cloth. Let rest for 30 minutes to 1 hour.

2 Divide the dough into six equal portions. Spread each piece into an oval. Apply a thin coating of oil on each oval and let rest for 30 minutes, covered with plastic wrap.

3 Take an oval, place it horizontally on the countertop and, with a chopstick, trace a horizontal line without cutting all the way through the dough. Holding both ends of the dough with your hands, pull it, stretching your hands as far as you can from each other. You should get a very long band (about 3½ feet or a little over 1 m). With your hands at one of the short ends of the dough, tear it vertically with your hands using a quick movement, giving you two long noodle bands. Repeat this process with the rest of the dough. Cook in boiling water for 2 to 3 minutes. Drain and serve with your choice of toppings.

TOMATO AND EGG NOODLES

Preparation: 10 minutes
Cooking time: 15 minutes

SERVES 2

- 6 cups (1.5 l) water
- 8.8 oz (250 g) fresh noodles of your choice (you can make the noodles yourself or use other types of Chinese noodles from the store)

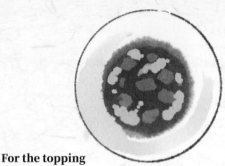

For the topping

- 2 eggs
- 1 green onion
- 3 medium tomatoes
- 2 tbsp. (30 ml) vegetable oil
- 2 tbsp. (30 ml) light soy sauce
- 2 tsp. (8.5 g) sugar
- ½ tsp. (2.5 g) salt
- Pepper to taste
- A few drops of sesame oil

1 In a bowl, beat the eggs. Chop the green onion. Wash the tomatoes and dice.

2 Heat the vegetable oil in a wok over high heat. Add the beaten eggs and stir with a pair of chopsticks or a fork to break up the omelet into small pieces. Transfer to a plate as soon as the eggs are not quite cooked through.

3 Place the tomatoes in the wok and cook until tender and juicy. Add the eggs, then add the green onion, soy sauce, sugar, salt and pepper. Continue cooking for 1 to 2 minutes over low heat so the eggs are saturated with tomato juice. Add a few drops of sesame oil at the end of the cooking.

4 Bring the water to a boil and cook the noodles for 2 to 3 minutes if fresh or according to the instructions on the packaging. Drain and combine with the tomato and egg mixture.

You can also add a little chili oil (p. 24) to spice up the dish.

JIAOZI

A *jiaozi* is a little dumpling with a dough made from wheat flour and stuffed with various ingredients such as meat, vegetables, fish or seafood. Originally from northern China, it is a dish for both big occasions and everyday meals. *Jiaozi* can be steamed, boiled or fried. Making *jiaozi* is a playful, fun and artistic endeavor.

捏饺子

Northeastern *jiaozi*

月儿饺

Half-moon *jiaozi*

麦穗饺

Leaf-shaped or wheat ear *jiaozi*

元宝饺

Gold ingot *jiaozi*

四喜饺

4-happiness *jiaozi*

锅贴

Guotie

虾饺

Har gow

DOUGH FOR BOILED JIAOZI

- 2 cups (250 g) all-purpose flour
- 1 pinch of salt
- ½ cup (125 ml) water

DOUGH FOR STEAMED OR FRIED JIAOZI

- 2 cups (250 g) all-purpose flour
- 1 pinch of salt
- ¾ cup (175 ml) boiling water

1 Place the flour and salt in a bowl, then gradually add the water, stirring with a pair of chopsticks or a fork to create small lumps.

2 Knead by hand for 5 minutes until the dough is smooth. Cover the dough with a damp cloth. Let rest at room temperature for 15 to 30 minutes before using.

MAKING DUMPLING WRAPPERS

With the dough, make a sausage shape. Cut the sausage into small pieces, like lozenges. Flatten each lozenge into a small circle. With a dumpling rolling pin, roll each circle of dough into a thin disk.

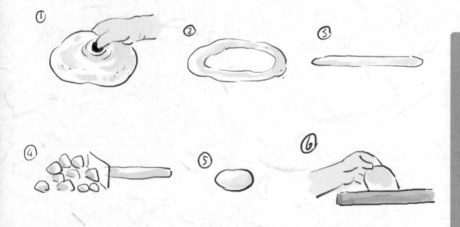

Don't make all the disks at once, as they could dry out. This is the best way to proceed. Make five or six disks, then make as many dumplings. Make five or six more disks before you go back to folding dumplings. Remember to generously flour the countertop when rolling out the disks.

NORTHEASTERN PORK JIAOZI

- ⅔ lb. (300 g) ground pork
- 1 tbsp. (15 ml) Shaoxing wine
- ½ tsp. (2 g) sugar
- 2 tbsp. (30 ml) light soy sauce
- 1.5-in. piece ginger, finely chopped
- 1 tbsp. (15 ml) sesame oil
- 2 medium leeks (only using the white parts of the leeks)
- 1 pinch of salt
- 2 tbsp. (30 ml) vegetable oil
- Dumpling wrappers (p. 55)

1 Combine the ground pork with the wine, sugar and soy sauce. Add the chopped ginger to the filling and stir. Add the sesame oil. Stir.

2 Slice the leek whites very thinly. Add to the filling and mix well. Add the salt, then the vegetable oil. Mix well.

3 Take the dumpling wrapper in your left hand, place 1 heaping teaspoon of filling in the center, then fold the dough in half to close it up by pressing each side with your thumb and index finger. Place each dumpling on a floured board. In a large saucepan, bring 6 cups (1.5 liters) of water to a boil. Place half the dumplings in the boiling water and cook for 5 to 6 minutes (once dumplings rise to the surface of the boiling water, cook for 1 minute longer). Remove the cooked dumplings with a slotted spoon and cook the other half of the dumplings.

VEGETARIAN GUOTIE (FRIED DUMPLINGS)

- 1¼ lb. (600 g) bok choy
- 2 oz (60 g) dried shiitake mushrooms
- 2 green onion
- 1.5-in. piece ginger
- 2 tsp. (10 ml) sesame oil
- 2 tbsp. (30 ml) vegetable oil
- Coarse salt
- Ground pepper
- 1 heaping tsp. (5 ml) flour
- 2½ cups (600 ml) water
- 1 tsp. (5 ml) black vinegar
- Vegetable oil for cooking
- Dumpling wrappers (p. 55)

1 Make the *guotie*: finely chop the bok choy, mushrooms, green onions, ginger, salt and pepper. Combine with the sesame and vegetable oils. Place 1 heaping teaspoon of filling in the center of each dumpling wrapper, bring the two sides to the middle and pinch tightly to close up. Leave the two ends slightly open so steam can escape during cooking.

2 Pour a thin coating of oil in a skillet and heat over high heat. Place the dumplings side by side in the skillet and brown for about 1 minute.

3 In a small bowl, combine the water, vinegar and flour. Pour this mixture in the skillet, cover and steam the dumplings for 7 to 8 minutes over medium heat until all of the liquid has evaporated. The bottoms of the dumplings will have a nice, golden crust as well as a crispy, lacy dumpling skirt.

DIM SUM

These dishes, often served as small bites, have been a great success around the world. Eating dim sum is always a congenial moment because you can enjoy a wide range of dishes with family or friends: steamed dumplings of all kinds, turnip or water chestnut cakes, buns stuffed with caramelized pork, small *bao* with tasty broth, fried spring rolls and desserts. There are so many options, it is impossible to mention them all.

Here are the most iconic dishes:

Ma lai gao: a sweet, very soft and light cake made of eggs and flour that is steamed.

Siu mai: these small, steamed bites are cork shaped with an opening at the top. They are often stuffed with pork, with the dough made from flour.

Har gow: steamed shrimp dumplings with transparent dough made from wheat starch.

Char siu bao: buns with fermented dough stuffed with Cantonese barbecued pork.

Spring rolls: fried rolls with vegetable, pork or shrimp fillings. The dough is made from flour.

Guotie or **fried dumplings**: although it is not a traditional dim sum dish, its great popularity often gives it a place on the menus of dim sum restaurants.

Xiao long bao: originally, these small, round, stuffed dumplings filled with a delicious broth were not a dim sum dish, but because people around the world like them so much, most dim sum restaurants now offer them.

BREADS

In China, there is an infinite number of foods made of leavened dough. They come in all sorts of shapes, textures and cooking methods, and they can be sweet, savory or plain.

Baozi: a small, steamed bun with a sweet or savory stuffing.

流沙包

Bao with a runny filling made of salted egg cream

核桃包

Nut-shaped bread

叉烧包

Char siu bao: steamed bread stuffed with glazed oven-roasted pork. This is a famous dim sum dish in Cantonese cuisine.

上海生煎包

Shanghai fried bao

蟹黄汤包

Bao with broth inside made from coral crab

小笼包

Xiao long bao: a small *bao* with pork broth

江苏三丁包

Jiangsu bao stuffed with chicken and bamboo shoots

新疆烤包子

Xinjiang baked *bao*

河南灌汤包

Henan *bao* with broth

四川韩包子

Sichuan *baozi* with sugar and lard in the dough

台湾刈包

Guabao: a small half-moon-shaped sandwich. The bread is steamed then filled with stewed pork belly. This is a Taiwanese specialty.

天津狗不理

Tianjin pork *baozi*

东北粘豆包

Bao made from millet

波萝油

Buttered pineapple bun

Hua juan: a small, twisted bun that can be plain, savory or sweet.

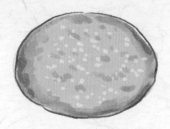

Nang: a large, round flat bread cooked in a traditional cylindrical charcoal oven. It's a Xinjiang specialty.

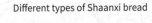

Flat bread cooked in a skillet or traditional oven

Different types of Shaanxi bread

Steamed longevity buns

Bing: a large, flaky bun that is cooked in a skillet. It can be plain, savory or lightly sweetened with a sesame sauce.

Rou jia mo: a small, round sandwich filled with pork stewed with spices and its juices. It is a specialty of Shaanxi and a form of street food known throughout China.

PORK AND LEEK BAOZI

Baozi are among the favorite street foods of Chinese people. These buns can be eaten at any time of day: for breakfast, at lunchtime, for a small snack...

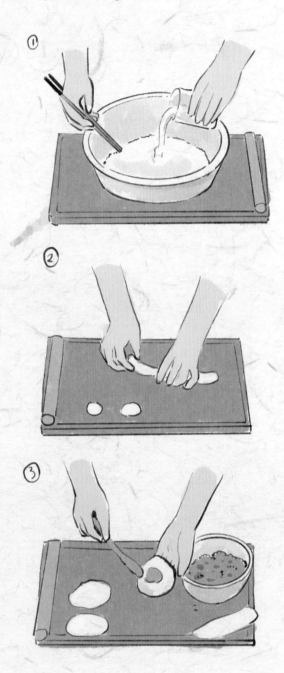

MAKES 15 BAOZI

For the dough
- 3½ cup (300 g) all-purpose flour
- 1½ tbsp. (22 ml) superfine sugar
- 1 tsp. (3 g) baker's yeast
- 6 oz (177 ml) warm water

For the filling: see the instructions for Northeastern pork *jiaozi* (p. 56).

1 Make the dough: In a large bowl, combine the flour and sugar. In another bowl, dilute the yeast with a little warm water and let the mixture bubble for 3 to 5 minutes. Gradually pour the yeast mixture over the flour while stirring. Add the rest of the warm water and stir. Knead the dough for 5 minutes until smooth. Cover with a damp tea towel and let rise for 1 to 1.5 hours in a warm place.

2 Fold the *bao*: With the dough, make a sausage shape, then tear it into equal portions. Make each piece into a small, flat shape. Roll out into disks that are 3¼ to 3½-in. (8 to 9 cm) in diameter. They should be ¼ in. (4 mm) thick in the center and ⅛ in. (2 mm) thick on the edges. Place 1 tablespoon of filling in the center of the disk. Hold the stuffed disk with your left hand. With your right index finger and thumb, pinch the right end to make the first fold. Place your left thumb inside the disk and press gently on the filling, with your left index finger outside. Push the top of the disk with your left index finger, then pinch with your right index finger and thumb to make the second fold over the first. Repeat, making 15 to 17 folds.

3 Place a piece of parchment paper with holes in it (made with scissors) in the steamer basket, then place the *bao* on top, spaced apart from each other. Cover and let rest 30 to 45 minutes (this second fermentation is very important, as it gives you a *bao* that is smooth and shiny). Half fill a saucepan (the same size as the steamer basket) with water. Place the steamer basket on the saucepan and bring the water to a boil. Reduce heat to low and cook for 15 minutes. Let rest 5 minutes before removing the lid.

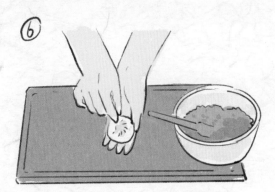

The original meaning of the word *baozi* is "small purse" or "small bag." For example, when you put together the characters for "silver" + "bao," this gives you the word "wallet." Similarly, "back" + "bao" makes the word "backpack."

The first *bao* appeared in the third century, in northern China, but at that time, it was called *mantou* or *momo* (a word still used today in Tibet for dumplings). It wasn't until the early 11th century that the word *bao* began to be used.

Traditionally, *bao* is eaten with a light soup, a soy drink or a broth.

RICE

Although a bowl of plain rice is a staple food in China, there are many other foods made from rice: fried rice, rice noodles, small pancakes, porridge, wide and flat noodles (like lasagna noodles), puffed rice, crispy rice and so on.

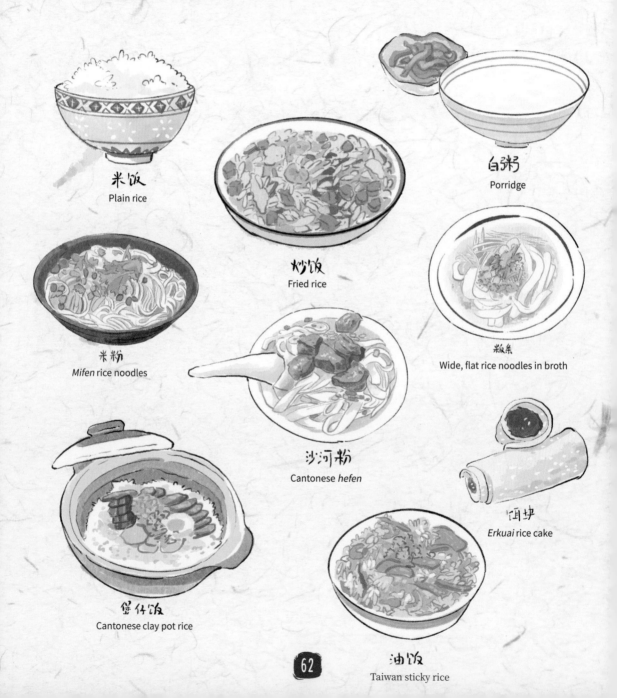

米饭
Plain rice

炒饭
Fried rice

白粥
Porridge

米粉
Mifen rice noodles

粄条
Wide, flat rice noodles in broth

沙河粉
Cantonese *hefen*

饵块
Erkuai rice cake

煲仔饭
Cantonese clay pot rice

油饭
Taiwan sticky rice

COOKING RICE STEP BY STEP

Preparation: 5 minutes
Cooking time: 20 minutes
Resting time: 10 minutes

SERVES 4

- 9 oz (250 g) short-grain rice
- 1½ cups (375 ml) water

淘米

1 Rinse the rice several times in water until the water becomes clear. Drain well between rinses. Add the rice to a saucepan or the inner pot of an electric rice cooker, add the water, then let the rice rest for 10 minutes. Bring to a boil and boil for around 3 minutes (when small holes form).

2 Cover, reduce heat to low and cook for 10 to 15 minutes. Turn off heat and let the rice rest for around 5 minutes.

> In China, the index finger is used to measure the amount of water to be added: with the tip of your finger touching the top surface of the rice, the level of water should be up to around your first knuckle. That's the right amount of water for any quantity of rice.

榨菜

Pickled mustard root

茶叶蛋

Tea eggs

CONGEE: PLAIN RICE PORRIDGE

SERVES 2 OR 3

- 2 oz. (60 g) short-grain rice or sushi rice
- 4 cups (1 l) water

咸蛋

Salted duck eggs

1 Rinse the rice several times in water, draining well between rinses.

2 In a saucepan, add the rice and the water and soak for 30 minutes.

3 Bring to a boil over high heat, then reduce heat to low and cook until the grains of rice are tender. Stir occasionally.

4 Serve the porridge with salted vegetables (such as pickled mustard root or dried fermented radishes), tea eggs or salted eggs.

FRIED RICE

Preparation: 10 minutes
Cooking time: 5 minutes

MAKES 4 BOWLS

- 2 eggs
- 3 green onions
- ¼ lb. (100 g) carrot
- 1 to 1.4 oz. (30 to 40 g) cured ham
- 3 tbsp. (45 ml) vegetable oil, divided
- 2 oz. (60 g) green peas
- 12 raw shrimp, shelled
- 1 tbsp. (15 ml) Shaoxing wine
- 1¾ cups (350 g) cooked rice
- Salt and ground white pepper to taste
- 1 tsp. (5 ml) sesame oil

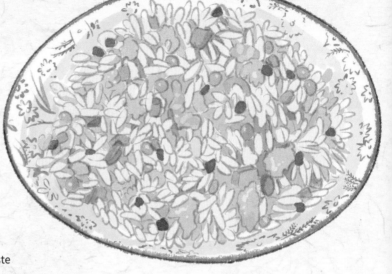

1 Beat the eggs. Slice the green onions, dice the carrot and cut the ham into small pieces.

2 Heat a wok with 1 tablespoon of oil over high heat. Stir fry the peas and diced carrot for 1 minute. Set aside.

3 Add 1 tablespoon of oil to the wok and stir fry the shrimp over high heat for 1 minute, add the Shaoxing wine and stir quickly. Add the ham and cook for 1 minute. Remove the cooked shrimp and ham from the wok and set aside.

4 Break up any large clumps of cooked rice — this is very important for a successful fried rice. Add the rice to the wok, over high heat. Add 1 tablespoon of oil and the beaten eggs, stirring immediately and constantly to blend well. Add the cooked vegetables, shrimp and ham to the wok and mix everything well. Add the green onions and the salt and pepper to taste. Stir the mixture for 1 minute, add a drizzle of sesame oil, stir again and serve.

Eggs
鸡蛋

Carrot
胡萝卜

Shrimp
虾仁

Cooked rice

Green peas
青豆

Cured ham
火腿

Green onion
葱花

STIR FRIED RICE NOODLES WITH BEEF

Preparation: 20 minutes
Cooking time: 10 minutes
Resting time: 15 minutes

SERVES 2

- 2 oz. (50 g) beef
- 1 + 2 tbsp. (15 ml + 30 ml) light soy sauce, divided
- 1 + 1 tsp. (5 ml + 5 ml) dark soy sauce
- 1 tsp. (4 g) potato starch
- 2 oz. (50 g) garlic chives
- 1 green onion
- ½ onion
- 2 tbsp. (30 ml) water
- 3 tbsp. (45 ml) vegetable oil, divided
- ½ lb. (200 g) fresh flat rice noodles
- 1 handful mung bean sprouts
- ½ tsp. (2.5 g) salt
- 1 tsp. (5 ml) sesame oil

1 Slice the beef thinly, about ⅟₁₆ in. (2 mm) thick, and mix with 1 tablespoon of light soy sauce, 1 teaspoon of dark soy sauce and the potato starch. Refrigerate for 15 minutes.

2 Slice the chives and green onion into 1½-in. (4-cm) sections. Julienne the onion. Mix the rest of the soy sauces with 2 tablespoons of water.

3 Heat 1½ tbsp (22 ml) of oil in the wok over high heat, sear the beef without stirring for 20 seconds, then stir gently until the meat changes color. Set the meat aside.

4 Heat the rest of the oil in the wok over high heat. Add the onion and green onion and stir fry for 20 to 30 seconds. Add the noodles and continue cooking for 1 to 2 minutes. Add the diluted soy sauces, stirring constantly. Add the bean sprouts, chives and salt, continue cooking for another 30 seconds, and then add the beef while still stirring. Remove from heat and add the sesame oil before serving.

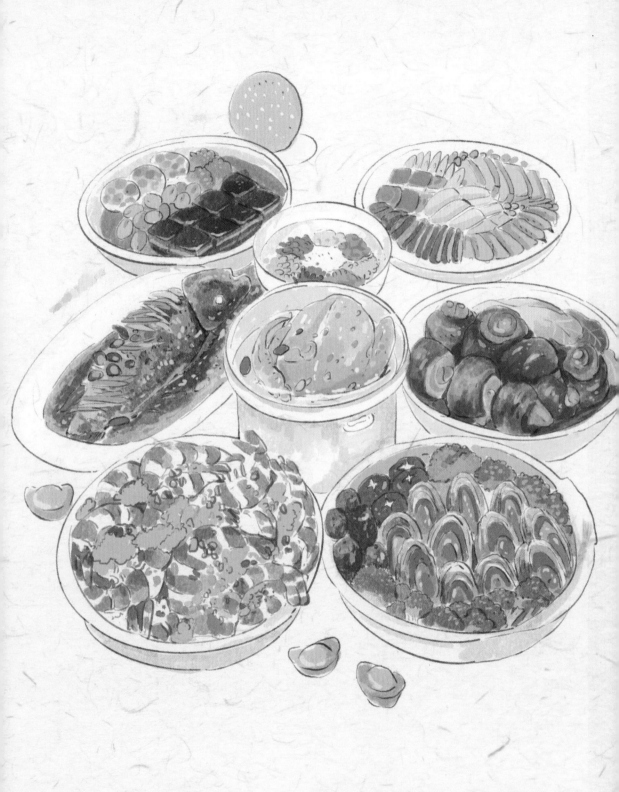

ESSENTIAL DISHES

Whether they are festive foods or
popular eats that are easy to make at home,
these essential dishes accompany the daily lives
of Chinese people. Eating is also an opportunity
to get together with family and friends.

PEKING DUCK, BEIJING KAOYA

When we talk about Chinese cooking, who doesn't think of Peking duck? Without a doubt, it is one of the most iconic dishes of this cuisine. Its complex preparation, its professional serving by a master carver and its ritual tasting make this a distinguished dish that people enjoy only in fine restaurants.

HISTORY

Peking duck was originally a dish from the imperial cuisine of the Ming dynasty. It was in modifying the Nanking duck recipe that Peking duck was created. When the Ming dynasty moved its capital from Nanking (now Nanjing) to Peking (now Beijing), this dish moved with it. Later, with the influence of Shandong cuisine (p. 36), green onion and the thin pancakes were introduced; these additions are part of Peking duck as we know it today.

Peking duck involves a long preparation that begins with the birth of the animal and involves cooking for several days: that is why it is expensive and almost impossible to make at home.

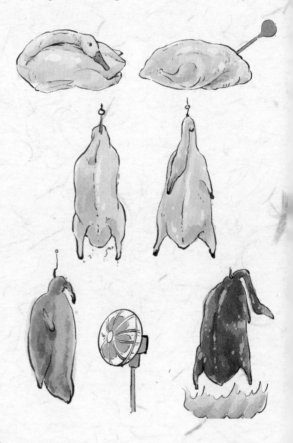

Traditionally, a White Pekin duck is used. The duckling is force fed for 60 to 70 days to fatten it, then its throat is cut when it has reached around 6 ½ lb. (3 kg). It must be butchered 24 to 48 hours before cooking. Next, through an incision made in its rump, it is inflated with air under the skin, which pulls away from the flesh. After the entrails are removed and the bird is scalded, it is coated with a mixture of honey and water, then hung in a well-ventilated room to dry. This gives it a nice blond caramel color, which will be enhanced during cooking.

The duck is roasted over a fire of fruit tree wood (like apple tree or jujube tree). The result is a duck with crispy, glistening skin and tender flesh thanks to the boiling water placed in the duck's stomach during cooking.

SERVICE

The duck, after being roasted, is carved in front of the guests by a Peking duck master carver. Traditionally, the duck is to be cut into exactly 108 slices, as 108 is a lucky number, but in practice, cutting around 100 slices is enough to give the meat a better texture. The skin from the breast is served separately; the crispy skin is a delicacy.

HOW TO EAT THE DUCK

Peking duck is eaten with thin pancakes made of flour, garnished with julienned green onion, cucumber and sweet bean (*tianmian jiang*) sauce (fermented and sweetened soybean paste).

Instructions: Take a crepe pancake. With your chopsticks, dip the julienned green onion in the *tianmian jiang* sauce, then place it on the pancake, add a stick of cucumber next to the green onion, add two or three pieces of meat, and then roll up the pancake and eat it with both hands while holding the bottom of the roll.

After the duck is eaten, guests are served a broth made from the duck carcass, which has simmered for a long time.

PORK

**Pork is the meat eaten most by Chinese people.
It can be used in many ways in all kinds of dishes!**

HONG SHAO PORK

This dish is made of pork belly that is simmered for a long time in soy sauce and caramelized — a typical dish in Hunan cuisine (p. 37). This was the favorite dish of Mao Zedong (the first president of the People's Republic of China).

Preparation: 15 minutes
Cooking time: 2 hours

SERVES 4

- 1¼ lb. (600 g) pork belly or pork shoulder
- 2 green onions
- 1.5-in. piece ginger
- 2 tbsp. (30 ml) light soy sauce
- 1 tbsp. (15 ml) dark soy sauce
- ¾ cup (200 ml) Shaoxing wine
- 1 oz. (25 g) rock sugar (bing tang)
- 1 tbsp. (15 ml) white rice vinegar (optional)

1 Cut the pork lengthwise, then in large pieces. In a saucepan, bring 1¼ cups (300 ml) of water to a boil, then blanch the meat for 2 minutes, skimming the surface. Drain.

2 Wash the green onions and cut in half. Peel the ginger and cut in strips. In a pan, brown the meat (without fat) for about 2 minutes. Add the two soy sauces and stir. Add the wine, then cover the meat with hot water. Add the ginger, green onions and rock sugar.

3 Stir and simmer over low heat for 1.5 to 2 hours, covered, until the meat is very tender. Reduce the sauce over high heat, stirring gently from time to time. When there is almost no sauce in the bottom of the pan, deglaze with the white rice vinegar and remove from heat.

LION'S HEAD MEATBALLS

五花肉

There is no lion meat in this dish, rather these are large pork meatballs that call to mind, according to Chinese people, the head of an imperial guardian lion. It is a specialty in Jiangsu and Zhejiang cuisine (p. 37).

Preparation: 20 minutes
Cooking time: 1 hour 45 minutes

SERVES 4 (12 LARGE MEATBALLS)

生抽 荸荠 鸡蛋 小白菜 姜 花雕酒

- 2-in. piece ginger
- 1 beaten egg
- 2 oz. (50 g) peeled water chestnuts (or lotus root)
- 1 lb. (500 g) ground pork shoulder
- ¼ lb. (100 g) minced pork belly
- 3 tbsp. (45 ml) Shaoxing wine
- 2 tbsp. (30 ml) light soy sauce
- Salt and pepper
- Cooking oil for frying
- ¼ lb. (100 g) bok choy
- 1 tbsp. (15 ml) vegetable oil

For the cooking sauce

- 2 green onions
- 1.5-in. piece ginger
- 1 tbsp. (15 ml) vegetable oil
- 1 tbsp. (15 ml) dark soy sauce
- 1 tbsp. (15 ml) light soy sauce
- 1 tbsp. (15 ml) Shaoxing wine
- 2 tsp. (10 ml) sugar
- Salt, to taste
- 2 cups (500 ml) hot water
- 2 tsp. (8 g) potato starch
- 3 tbsp. (45 ml) water

1 To make the meatballs, chop the ginger, beat the egg and coarsely chop the water chestnuts. In a large bowl, combine the pork with the Shaoxing wine, soy sauce, ginger and egg. Add salt and pepper, then the water chestnuts. Mix well. Make large meatballs from this mixture (about 1¾ oz. [50 g] per meatball). In a wok, heat the cooking oil to 320°F (160°C). Add the meatballs one at a time without moving them at first, and when they are lightly browned, drain and set aside.

2 Wash the bok choy and cut in large pieces. Stir fry over high heat in a wok with 1 tablespoon of vegetable oil. Remove and set aside.

3 Make the sauce: Chop the green onions and slice the ginger finely. Place 1 tablespoon of vegetable oil in a saucepan and brown the ginger and green onions over medium heat for 1 minute. Add the soy sauces, Shaoxing wine and sugar, and continue cooking while stirring for 1 minute. Pour 2 cups (500 ml) of hot water into the pan. Add a pinch of salt, then the meatballs. Bring to a boil, reduce heat and simmer for 1 hour, covered. Stir the meatballs occasionally. Add the bok choy 5 minutes before the end of cooking.

4 In a dish, arrange the bok choy, then place the meatballs on top (without the sauce).

5 In a bowl, combine the potato starch with 3 tablespoons of water. Bring the sauce to a boil, add the starch mixture and stir right away. When the sauce thickens, pour it over the meatballs and serve.

CHICKEN

In China, chicken is cooked in different ways depending on its sex, age and breed.
For example, a hen that no longer lays eggs is excellent for making a broth.
In the north, a young rooster is often stewed with mushrooms.

IMPERIAL CHICKEN

Preparation: 15 minutes
Marinating time: 30 minutes
Cooking time: 10 minutes

SERVES 4

- ½ lb. (250 g) chicken breast or chicken thigh meat
- 1 oz. (30 g) raw skinned peanuts
- 1 tbsp. + 1 tbsp. (15 ml + 15 ml) sunflower oil
- 1 green onion
- 6 or 7 dried chili peppers
- 1 garlic clove
- 2 strips ginger
- 1 tsp. (5 g) Sichuan pepper

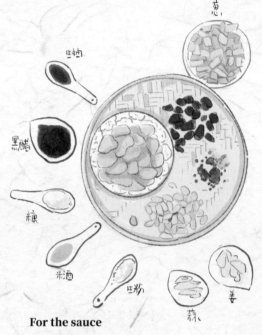

For the marinade

- 1 tbsp. (15 ml) Shaoxing wine
- 1 tbsp. (15 ml) light soy sauce
- 1 tsp. (4 g) potato starch

For the sauce

- 1 tsp. (4 g) potato starch
- 1 tsp. (4 g) sugar
- 5 tbsp. (75 ml) water
- 1 tbsp. (15 ml) light soy sauce
- 2 tsp. (10 ml) rice vinegar

1 Cut the chicken in strips lengthwise, then cut into small cubes.

2 Make the marinade. In a bowl, combine the Shaoxing wine and soy sauce. Add the cubed chicken. Add the potato starch and stir. Knead the chicken cubes to saturate them with marinade. Refrigerate for 30 minutes. Meanwhile, toast the peanuts in a skillet over low heat with 1 tablespoon of sunflower oil. Place the toasted peanuts on a paper towel. Wash the green onion and cut into disks. Cut the dried chili peppers into small pieces. Peel and chop the garlic. Chop the ginger.

3 In a bowl, combine all the sauce ingredients. Set aside.

4 Heat the rest of the oil in a wok, then stir fry the dried chili peppers and Sichuan pepper for 1 minute over medium heat. Set aside on a plate. Place the marinated chicken cubes in the wok and sear 2 to 3 minutes over high heat. Add the ginger, garlic and green onion. Stir the sauce vigorously, then pour it into the wok. Mix rapidly. The sauce will be ready in less than 30 seconds. Add the dried chili peppers, Sichuan pepper and peanuts. Mix and serve right away.

THREE CUP CHICKEN

Originally, this was a Jiangxi dish made with chicken, a cup of rice wine, a cup of soy sauce and a cup of sesame oil. The version eaten today is the Taiwanese one, which includes a new ingredient: Thai basil leaves.

Preparation: 10 minutes
Cooking time: 1 hour 30 minutes

SERVES 4

- 2 lb. (800 g) free-range yellow chicken, cut in pieces
- 3-in. piece ginger
- 2 green onions
- 4 garlic cloves
- ¾ cup (200 ml) Shaoxing wine
- 3½ tbsp. (50 ml) light soy sauce
- 3½ tbsp. (50 ml) dark soy sauce
- 3½ tbsp. (50 ml) hot water
- ¾ oz. (20 g) rock sugar (bing tang)
- 2 tbsp. (30 ml) sesame oil
- Salt

1 In a large saucepan, sear the chicken pieces, skin side down (add a drizzle of oil if the chicken is lean).

2 Meanwhile, peel the ginger, then cut it and the green onions into large pieces. Peel the garlic cloves. When the chicken pieces are browned on all sides, add the ginger, garlic cloves and green onions. Continue cooking for 1 minute while stirring.

3 Add the wine, two soy sauces, hot water and rock sugar. Mix well. Turn heat to low and steam for 1 to 1.5 hours.

4 At the end of the cooking time, turn up the heat to reduce the sauce, stirring occasionally. Add sesame oil and salt to taste and stir.

For the Taiwanese version, brown a little chili pepper at the beginning of the cooking process and add a few fresh Thai basil leaves at the end.

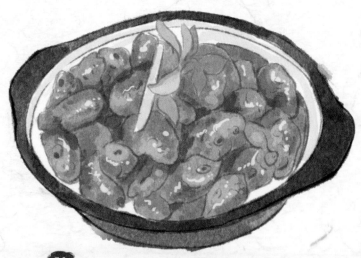

FISH AND SEAFOOD

The Chinese word for fish is pronounced the same way as the word for abundance. Fish are therefore a symbol of bounty in China. At the table, fish is often served whole, which means a whole year of abundance, from beginning to end!

STEAMED SEA BASS

Preparation: 15 minutes
Cooking time: 15 minutes

SERVES 4

- 1 2 lb 4 oz. (1 kg) sea bass, cleaned and scaled
- 5 tsp. (25 ml) Shaoxing wine
- Salt and ground black pepper
- 4.5-in. piece ginger
- 2 green onions
- 3 tbsp. (45 ml) light soy sauce
- 4 tbsp. (60 ml) vegetable oil

1 Rinse the sea bass. Place it on the countertop, then make four or five parallel vertical slits on each side of the fish. Drizzle the sea bass with the wine, rubbing it into the flesh so it soaks in. Add salt and pepper.

2 Cut half the ginger into thin disks. Arrange on the belly of the fish. Place the fish in a large steamer and cook 10 to 15 minutes once the water comes to a boil. Meanwhile, julienne the rest of the ginger and the green onions. Remove the cooked fish and place it gently on a heat-proof plate. Sprinkle with the julienned ginger. Season with soy sauce and sprinkle with green onion. Meanwhile, heat the oil in a saucepan over high heat. When it starts to smoke, pour it evenly over the fish. Serve immediately.

STEAMED SHRIMP

Preparation: 15 minutes
Marinating: 30 minutes
Cooking time: 5 minutes

SERVES 4

- 2 oz. (50 g) mung bean vermicelli
- 8 large raw, unpeeled shrimp
- 2 tbsp. (30 ml) Shaoxing wine
- 3 or 4 garlic cloves
- 5 tbsp. (75 ml) vegetable oil
- 4 tbsp. (60 ml) light soy sauce

1 Soak the vermicelli in a bowl of hot water (around 140°F or 60°C) for 30 minutes. Remove the legs and the antennae from the shrimp. Make a slit on the back of each shrimp and devein. Place the shrimp on a plate, drizzle with the wine and salt lightly.

2 Crush the garlic cloves and grind it into a puree. Brown the garlic paste in a saucepan with the oil for 5 minutes over medium heat. Place this garlic puree and its oil in a small bowl. Add the soy sauce and stir. Drain the vermicelli and arrange in a dish that can go in the steamer. Add a little garlic sauce, then arrange the shrimp on top. Brush the shrimp with the garlic sauce. Place the dish in the steamer and cook 5 minutes over high heat once the water starts boiling. Serve immediately.

HAIRY CRAB

The name "hairy crab" comes from the fact that part of its claws and legs are covered in small, soft hairs. They are also known as "Chinese mitten crabs." The best time to eat these crabs is from autumn to the beginning of winter. This is a delicacy using a very simple cooking method, such as steaming or boiling in water. Traditionally, it is eaten with a sauce made of vinegar and fresh ginger, a glass of warm Shaoxing wine or an infusion made with ginger and black sugar 姜母茶 (p. 123). Because crab is known as a yin (cold) food, it should be eaten with yang (hot) foods, such as ginger and wine.

SERVES 4

- 4 Chinese mitten crabs
- 10½ cups (2.5 l) water
- 3 tbsp. (45 ml) Shaoxing wine
- A few shiso leaves (optional)

For the sauce

- 4.5-in. piece ginger, finely chopped
- 8 tbsp. (120 ml) black vinegar
- 4 tbsp. (60 ml) light soy sauce

1 Wash and scrub the crabs well. In a stock pot, bring water to a boil. Add the crabs, wine and shiso leaves, and let the water return to a boil. Cover and cook for 10 to 12 minutes.

2 In a bowl, combine all the ingredients for the sauce. Steep for a little while.

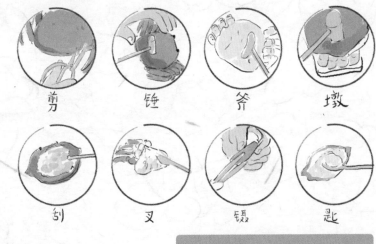

Some Chinese people use an eight-piece set of tools to eat the crabs so that their fingers don't get dirty.

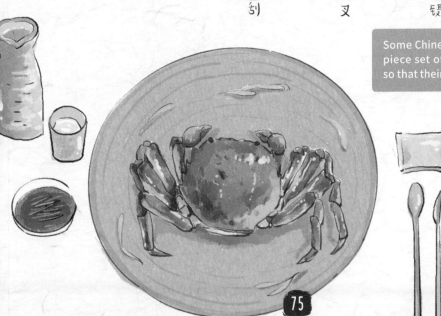

EGGS AND TOFU

TOMATO EGG STIR FRY

Preparation: 5 minutes
Cooking time: 10 minutes

SERVES 4

- 4 eggs
- 2 tsp. (10 ml) Shaoxing wine
- 1 green onion
- 5 medium tomatoes
- 3 tbsp. (45 ml) vegetable oil
- 1 tbsp. (12 g) superfine sugar
- 1 tbsp. (15 ml) light soy sauce
- Salt and ground black pepper

1 In a bowl, beat the eggs with the wine. Wash the green onion and slice finely. Wash the tomatoes and cut them into wedges. Heat the oil in a wok over high heat. Add the beaten eggs and stir with a pair of chopsticks or a fork to break up the omelet into small pieces. Transfer the eggs to a plate when they are still runny.

2 Place the tomatoes in the wok, add the soy sauce and cook until tender and juicy. Return the eggs to the wok, then add the green onion, sugar, salt and pepper. Continue cooking for 1 to 2 minutes over low heat until the eggs are saturated with the tomato juice. Serve immediately.

TEA EGGS

Preparation: 5 minutes
Cooking time: 20 minutes
Resting time: 48 hours

茶叶蛋

SERVES 5

- 5 eggs
- 2 cups (500 ml) hot water
- 2 to 3 tsp. (4–6 g) red tea leaves

- 1 tsp. (5 g) Sichuan pepper
- 1 star anise
- 2 tsp. (10 g) salt

1 In a saucepan, bring 4 cups (1 l) of water to a boil. Immerse the eggs and cook for 5 minutes.

2 Run them under cold water, then make small cracks on the shell with a spoon or by rolling them gently on the countertop.

3 Pour 2 cups (500 ml) of hot water into the pan; add the red tea leaves, Sichuan pepper, star anise and salt.

4 Place the cracked eggs in this mixture and cook over medium heat for 15 minutes.

5 Remove from heat and leave the eggs in the infusion for 48 hours.

6 Drain the eggs, gently peel and serve.

MAPO TOFU

Preparation: 20 minutes
Cooking time: 20 minutes

SERVES 4

- 2 lb. (800 g) firm tofu
- 1.5-in. piece ginger
- 2 garlic cloves
- 2 green onions
- 3 tbsp. (45 ml) vegetable oil
- 2 tbsp. (30 ml) *doubanjiang*
- 2 tbsp. (30 g) fermented black soybeans
- 2 ¼ cups (550 ml) warm water or chicken broth

- 2 tsp. (8 g) potato starch
- 7 tbsp. (100 ml) water
- 2 tsp. (8 g) super-fine sugar
- 2 tsp. (10 g) ground Sichuan pepper
- 2 tsp. (6 g) chili powder
- 2 tsp. (10 ml) light soy sauce

1 Drain the tofu, then cut it into 1-in. (2-cm) cubes.

2 Bring a saucepan of salted water to a boil. Immerse the tofu cubes in the boiling water for 1 minute, then run under cold water. Drain.

3 Peel and finely chop the ginger and garlic.

4 Wash and slive the green onions. Heat the oil in a wok over medium heat. Add the *doubanjiang* and black soybeans, then stir.

5 Add the ginger, green onions and chopped garlic, then continue cooking for 1 to 2 minutes.

6 Add the warm water (or chicken broth) and bring to a boil. Lower the heat and add the tofu cubes. Cover and simmer for 3 minutes.

7 In a bowl, dilute the potato starch with the water. Turn the heat under the wok to high, then add the diluted starch, stirring gently.

8 When the mixture has thickened, add the sugar, Sichuan pepper, chili powder and soy sauce. Mix well and remove from heat.

Soy beverage

Tofu strips

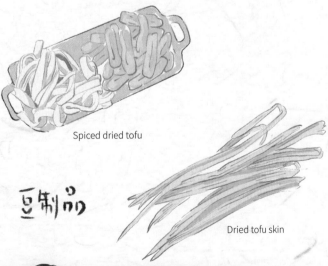

Spiced dried tofu

豆制品

Dried tofu skin

VEGETABLES

CABBAGE

Cabbage is the most commonly eaten vegetable in China. There are many varieties, including Napa cabbage, *bok choy*, *choy sum* and round cabbage.

Napa cabbage

大白菜

Shanghai bok choy

上海青

Round cabbage

包菜

Dwarf bok choy

奶白菜

SPICY CABBAGE STIR FRY

SERVES 4

- ¾ lb (350 g) round cabbage
- 1 garlic clove
- 1.5-in. piece ginger
- 2 tbsp. (30 ml) vegetable oil
- 1 tsp. (5 g) Sichuan pepper
- 4 small dried chili peppers
- 2 tbsp. (30 ml) light soy sauce
- 1 tbsp. (15 ml) black vinegar
- ½ tsp. (2 g) potato starch
- 1 tbsp. (15 ml) water
- 1 pinch of sugar
- 1 tsp. (5 ml) sesame oil

1 Tear the cabbage leaves with your hands. Chop the garlic and ginger.

2 Heat the oil over high heat in a wok. Add the Sichuan pepper, dried chili peppers, garlic and ginger, and stir fry for 20 to 30 seconds. Add the cabbage leaves. Mix well.

3 Combine the soy sauce and vinegar in a small bowl. Add a little water for a total of ⅓ cup (75 ml) of liquid. Add this mixture around the sides of the wok. Stir well.

4 Combine the potato starch with 1 tablespoon of water and a pinch of sugar. When the cabbage leaves start to soften, add the starch mixture, stirring constantly until the mixture is thickened. Then add the sesame oil, stir and serve.

EGGPLANT

Many kinds of eggplant can be found in China. The long and thin ones are used most often.

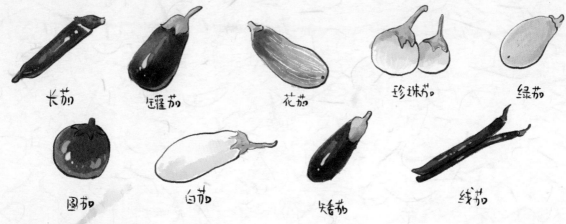

长茄　　　垩蘿茄　　　花茄　　　珍珠茄　　　绿茄

圆茄　　　白茄　　　矢香茄　　　线茄

SICHUAN EGGPLANT YU XIANG

Yu xiang is a mixture of ingredients in a sauce that has a vinegary, sweet, spicy flavor. Originally, this sauce was used for preparing fish in Sichuan.

SERVES 4
- 14–17½ oz. (400–500 g) eggplant
- 3–4 garlic cloves
- 1 green onion
- 2-in. piece ginger
- 3–4 tbsp. (45–60 ml) vegetable oil

For the sauce
- 1 tbsp. (15 ml) *doubanjiang*
- ½ tbsp. (6.5 g) sugar
- 1 tsp. (4 g) potato starch
- 5–6 tbsp. (75–90 ml) water
- 1 tbsp. (15 ml) black vinegar
- 1 tbsp. (15 ml) light soy sauce

1 Cut the unpeeled eggplants into pieces. Salt and let rest for 30 minutes. Squeeze the eggplants well to remove the water. Chop the garlic, green onion and ginger.

2 Heat the oil in a wok over high heat, add the eggplant pieces and stir fry for about 3 minutes. Add the garlic, green onion and ginger. Reduce heat and continue cooking for 2 to 3 minutes over low heat, until the eggplant pieces are soft.

3 Combine all the sauce ingredients in a bowl. Remove the eggplant pieces from the wok and set aside. Over high heat, add the sauce to the wok, stirring constantly until the sauce has thickened. Return the eggplant to the wok and stir quickly without breaking up the eggplant pieces. Serve.

LEAFY GREEN VEGETABLES

Chinese people are big fans of leafy green vegetables known for their health benefits, their freshness and their simple cooking methods.

These are the best known and most consumed:

· water spinach
· baby spinach
· amaranth leaves

· edible chrysanthemum leaves
· Chinese broccoli.

WATER SPINACH STIR FRIED WITH GARLIC

Water spinach is a favorite vegetable among Chinese people. Cooking it is simple: Blanch and serve with a sauce, or cook quickly in a wok with crushed garlic, sometimes with chili peppers or a sauce made of fermented tofu.

Preparation: 5 minutes
Cooking time: 5 minutes

MAKES 4 SMALL SERVINGS
· 1 lb. (400 g) water spinach
· 2 garlic cloves
· 2 tbsp. (30 ml) vegetable oil
· Salt

1 Wash the water spinach and cut in pieces 1½ to 2 in. (4 to 5 cm) long. Peel and chop the garlic.

2 Heat the oil over medium heat in a wok. Add the chopped garlic then the water spinach, stir quickly and add salt. When the water spinach is wilted, remove from heat and serve.

SPINACH SALAD WITH VERMICELLI

Preparation: 5 minutes
Cooking time: 6 minutes
Resting time: 30 minutes

SERVES 2

- ½ lb. (200 g) spinach
- 2 oz. (50 g) mung bean vermicelli
- 4 cups (1 l) simmering water

For the sauce
- 1.5-in. piece ginger with skin
- 2 tbsp. (30 ml) light soy sauce

- 1 tbsp. (15 ml) white rice vinegar
- 1 tbsp. (15 ml) sesame oil

1 Wash the spinach.

2 Simmer the vermicelli for 5 minutes in 4 cups (1 l) of water. Remove and keep the simmering water. Place the cooked vermicelli in cold water, then drain.

3 Simmer the spinach in the simmering water for about 20 seconds. Remove and drain. Combine the vermicelli with the spinach.

4 Grate the ginger into a puree. Combine all the sauce ingredients in a small bowl, then pour over the vermicelli-spinach mixture. Mix well and let the dish rest 30 minutes before serving.

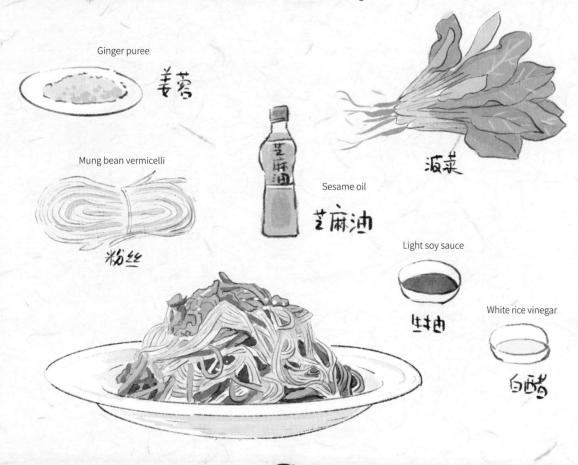

Ginger puree
姜蓉

Mung bean vermicelli
粉丝

Sesame oil
芝麻油

波菜

Light soy sauce
生抽

White rice vinegar
白醋

SOUPS

Daily meals often end with a quickly prepared light soup. The soup ingredients change with the seasons: cabbage in winter, spinach or baby lettuce in spring, tomato or cucumber in summer and so on.

TOMATO SOUP

Preparation: 5 minutes
Cooking time: 10 minutes

SERVES 4

- 2 medium tomatoes
- 1 green onion
- 2 eggs

- 3 ¾ cup (900 ml) water
- Salt and ground white pepper
- 2 or 3 drops of sesame oil

1 Wash the tomatoes and cut into sections. Wash the green onion and slice. Beat the eggs in a bowl.

2 Pour the water into a saucepan and bring to a boil. Add the tomatoes, reduce heat and simmer for 2 minutes. Add salt and pepper. Remove from heat and add the beaten eggs in a thin stream while stirring with chopsticks. Add the green onion and sesame oil. Serve immediately.

SUAN LA TANG
(HOT AND SOUR SOUP)

Soaking time: overnight
Preparation: 25 minutes
Cooking time: 20 minutes

SERVES 4

- 1 oz. (25 g) dried shiitake mushrooms
- ¼ oz. (7 g) dried wood ear mushrooms
- 5 oz. (150 g) bamboo shoots
- 2 tsp. (4 g) potato starch
- 6½ oz. (200 ml) water to dilute the starch
- ¼ lb. (100 g) carrot
- 1 egg
- 1 green onion
- ½ oz. (15 g) fresh cilantro stems
- 1 tbsp. (15 ml) vegetable oil
- 2 tbsp. (30 ml) light soy sauce
- 3⅓ cup (800 ml) water for the soup
- 1 tsp. (5 ml) chili paste
- 1 to 2 heaping tsp. (5–10 g) ground white pepper
- 3 tbsp. (45 ml) black vinegar
- A few fresh cilantro leaves

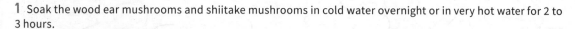

1 Soak the wood ear mushrooms and shiitake mushrooms in cold water overnight or in very hot water for 2 to 3 hours.

2 Rinse the bamboo shoots under cold water several times, then quickly immerse them in boiling water. Drain well and set aside.

3 Dilute the potato starch in 6½ oz. (200 ml) of water. Julienne the carrots. Beat the egg.

4 Slice the shiitakes into thin strips, and cut the wood ear mushrooms and bamboo shoots into small pieces. Chop the green onion and cilantro stems. Set the cilantro stems aside.

5 Heat a wok or pot over medium heat, add the oil, then add the chopped green onion, shiitakes, wood ear mushrooms and bamboo shoots. Stir fry with the light soy sauce for 3 to 4 minutes.

6 Add the julienned carrots, then continue cooking for 2 minutes. Turn heat to high, add 3⅓ cups (800 ml) of hot water, add the chili paste and the pepper, and bring to a boil. Add the starch mixture. Stir the mixture constantly until thickened.

7 Reduce heat a little; gradually add the beaten egg in a circular motion; do not stir right away. Add the chopped cilantro stems and vinegar, and stir gently.

8 Remove from heat and add a few cilantro leaves before serving.

HOTPOT

**Chinese hotpot is a wonderful meal to share with friends or family.
There are many different types of hotpots in China depending on the region:
Beijing lamb hotpot from Inner Mongolia, spicy Sichuan hotpot,
Cantonese hotpot, Yunnan mushroom hotpot and many more.**

Hotpot consists of a simmering broth and raw foods to be cooked at the table during the meal. For this à-la-carte dish, you can vary the type of broth and the foods you include depending on your tastes and your mood.

Equipment needed: A hotplate or a special hotpot cooker, a pot for cooking the ingredients, small cups for the sauces, bowls for the broth, chopsticks and a slotted spoon to remove the food from the broth.

Broth: There are many types of broth. The most basic one is chicken broth. If you like more intense flavors, you can make a spicy Sichuan broth. For Mongolian hotpot, you just need boiling water with a little green onion and ginger.

MUSHROOM HOTPOT

Soaking time: 30 minutes
Preparation: 30 minutes
Cooking time: 5 minutes

SERVES 4

- ⅓ oz. (12 g) dried shiitake mushrooms
- ¼ oz. (8 g) dried wood ear mushrooms
- 2 oz. (50 g) mung bean vermicelli
- ⅓ lb. (150 g) bok choy
- ½ lb. (200 g) white radishes
- 1.5-in. piece ginger
- 3 green onions
- ½ lb. (200 g) white mushrooms

- ⅓ lb. (150 g) shimeji mushrooms
- ¼ lb. (100 g) enoki mushrooms
- 1 tbsp. (15 ml) vegetable oil
- 1 star anise
- 2 oz. (50 g) bamboo shoots
- 4 cups (1 l) chicken broth
- 2 to 4 cups (0.5–1 l) spring water
- Salt
- 2 oz. (60 g) Chinese noodles

For the sauce

- 1½ tbsp. (22 ml) sesame paste
- 3½ tbsp. (50 ml) warm water
- 2 tbsp. (30 ml) light soy sauce
- 1 tbsp. (15 ml) black vinegar
- 1 tsp. (5 ml) spicy oil or/and sesame oil
- 1 pinch of sugar
- Salt

1 Soak the shiitake and wood ear mushrooms in hot water separately for at least 30 minutes. Soak the vermicelli in warm water for 30 minutes.

2 Wash and spin the bok choy. Peel the white radishes and slice finely. Slice the ginger and chop the green onions. Slice the white mushrooms. Pull apart the shimeji and enoki mushrooms.

3 Place all ingredients on several plates.

4 Drain the vermicelli and place it in a large bowl or plate.

5 Heat the oil in a pot. Add the ginger, green onions and star anise. Brown for 1 minute over medium heat. Add the shiitakes and bamboo shoots and cook for 1 minute. Add the broth and water and bring to a boil, then reduce heat to low. Salt lightly. Simmer for 15 to 30 minutes.

6 Meanwhile, place all the sauce ingredients in a bowl. Mix well.

7 Place the pot on a portable hot plate on the table and bring to a boil.

8 Now you can cook whatever you like in the pot!

9 The noodles can be cooked first as they require the most cooking time.

10 For the mushrooms and vegetables, 30 seconds is plenty.

11 Dip the cooked foods in sauce. At the end, you can drink the broth, which has absorbed all the flavors. It is delightful!

MAJOR THEMES

In China, cooking goes well beyond supplying nutrients: It plays an essential role in the life of each person.

In this chapter we will explore:

· The link between health and diet, as a taste of Chinese philosophy;

· Vegetarian cooking, which is joy-filled and creative;

· Symbolic foods served for everyday meals or for celebrations;

· Street food, which gives a rhythm to life in China.

HEALTH AND FOOD

A Chinese proverb says that "food and remedies have the same source." This means that foods have the same virtues as Chinese remedies. When we get sick, the first thing to do is change our diet; when we're in good health, respecting balance by maintaining healthy eating is essential for staying well.

YANG SHENG

Yang sheng literally means "nourishing life." It is the art of eating the right foods at the right time, which allows each person to stay well and improve their longevity.

In the philosophy of *yang sheng*, we seek harmony and well-being within the body. Food is essential, because it is one of the main causes of blocked energy (*qi*) in our body. We must eat well, in moderation, while observing the state of our body and its environment. Here are a few ground rules:

· Avoid raw and cold foods;
· Avoid wet dairy products and refined sugars;
· Take your time and chew to encourage predigestion;
· Eat more vegetables and grains, and eat meat and fish in small quantities;
· Stop eating when you are full.

It is also important to connect with the rhythm of the *jieqi*, the 24 moments in the traditional calendar (p. 42–45) related to the rhythm of the sun, and to do physical exercises to boost your energy.

When people cough in the fall, they make a stewed pear soup to treat the respiratory system.

During summer heatwaves, Chinese people often eat mung bean soup, which helps to lower body temperature and has detoxifying properties.

CHINESE MEDICINE

Chinese medicine, like Chinese cooking, seeks harmony. In cooking, we seek harmony between flavors, textures, colors, etc., and in medicine, we aim to maintain harmony in the energy within the body as well as between the body and external elements.

THE FIVE FLAVORS: ACIDIC, SWEET, BITTER, SPICY AND SALTY

Foods are organized into five flavors, in relation to the seasons and the five elements (metal, wood, water, fire and earth).

In Chinese medicine, flavor is considered through an energy lens; it has nothing to do with how food tastes. Some foods can have several flavors at the same time. Each flavor is linked to an element, a season and an organ upon which it acts.

Eaten in reasonable quantities, each flavor invigorates the organ associated with it. But if there is too much, it can have harmful effects. For example, acid nourishes the liver, but it can also hurt muscles and tendons and cause cramps and tendinitis.

Acidic	Sweet	Bitter	Spicy	Salty
酸	甜	苦	辛	咸
Lemon	Cabbage	Amaranth leaf	Ginger	Seaweed
Plum	Spinach	Bitter cucumber	Cilantro	Pork
Pomegranate	Banana	Lotus seeds	Green onion	Fish

THE FOUR NATURES OF FOODS: COLD, COOL, WARM AND HOT

The four natures have a real thermal effect on the body. Through eating, and especially thanks to the nature of foods, we can influence our thermal balance based on our needs.

For example, duck has a cool nature and is best eaten in summer; lamb has a warm nature, suitable for winter; apples have a warm nature and sweet taste and are best eaten in winter...

In Chinese medicine, digestion is compared to a pot on the stove; for digestion to go well, it needs heat. For example, if we eat too many cool or cold foods, this can slow down the process, which slows down or even blocks the metabolic system.

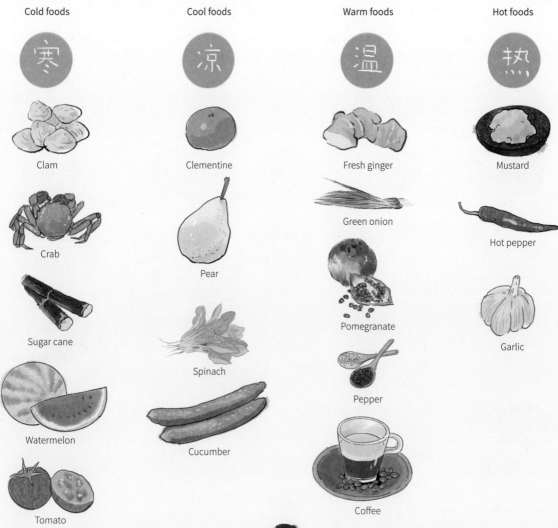

Cold foods 寒
- Clam
- Crab
- Sugar cane
- Watermelon
- Tomato

Cool foods 凉
- Clementine
- Pear
- Spinach
- Cucumber

Warm foods 温
- Fresh ginger
- Green onion
- Pomegranate
- Pepper
- Coffee

Hot foods 执
- Mustard
- Hot pepper
- Garlic

YIN AND YANG

The principle of *yin* and *yang* comes from Taoist philosophy, in the *I Ching*, or *Book of Changes*.

The symbol of *yin* and *yang* is well known around the world. *Yin*, shown in black, evokes, among other things, femininity, the moon, darkness, coolness, receptivity, etc. *Yang*, shown in white, represents masculinity, the sun, light, heat, momentum, action, etc.

The basic idea behind *yin* and *yang* is fairly simple: Everything in the world has a necessary opposite pole. According to this philosophy, the two opposing forces are constantly alternating: a high phase is followed by a low phase, movement is followed by rest, and so on, just as night follows day and the sun follows the moon.

Foods are also a source of *yin* and *yang* according to their place on the spectrum, whose two poles are *yin* and *yang*.

Among *yin* food sources — feminine, moist and soft — we find most vegetables and fruits. Meanwhile, *yang* food sources are masculine: fried, spicy or meat based.

VEGETARIAN CUISINE

CREATIVE VEGETARIAN CUISINE

Although meat is available to everyone in China today, this was not the case for the three previous generations. At that time, meat dishes were reserved for special occasions. This lack of meat fostered a diet that contained a lot more vegetables, mushrooms and tofu, leading to an extremely creative vegetarian cuisine. Cooks mastered the use of products such as wheat protein (seitan) or soy to make dishes imitating the flavor, shape and texture of meat. Among the most popular are vegetarian meatballs, vegetarian fish, sweet and sour vegetarian filet mignon and stewed vegetarian pork belly. At times, the dishes look much like their meat equivalents. Many of these recipes are part of Chinese tradition and are highly acclaimed.

Vegetarian fried fish made with mushrooms

Vegetarian pork belly

Sweet and sour vegetarian filet mignon

INGREDIENTS USED IN VEGETARIAN COOKING

Tofu

Seitan

Fried tofu skin

Dried tofu skin

Soybeans

Red beans (adzuki)

Mung beans

Seaweed

Fresh bean curd skin

Black soybeans

Edamame

TEMPLE CUISINE (ZHAI CAI)

Buddhism and Taoism are the two main religions in China. Both are founded on principles of compassion and harmony, and both influenced the nation's first vegetarian tendencies.

Buddhist cuisine is vegetarian, but it does not use certain vegetables (garlic, green onions, chives, shallots) because these strong-smelling foods are thought to stimulate the senses, disrupting meditation.

Today, many temples throughout the country also serve vegetarian meals and are open to the public.

Bowl of noodles in a temple in Suzhou.

SYMBOLIC FOODS

For Chinese people, a food does not just contain nutrients; it also has symbolic value. For every special occasion celebrated around a meal, foods are chosen based on symbols that correspond to the event.

In China, the relationship between a food and its symbolic meaning generally comes from a close pronunciation of the two words in Chinese. For example, chicken is *ji* in Chinese; it is pronounced the same way as the word for "good omen." A pear is not shared with another person, because "sharing the pear" is pronounced the same way as the word "separation" (*fenli*).

FOR CELEBRATING BIRTHDAYS
过生日

Noodles are an essential dish for birthdays because their length is the symbol of longevity. When an older person is celebrating a birthday, steamed buns in the shape of a peach — a fruit that symbolizes a good omen and longevity — are also served.

OTHER FOODS WITH PARTICULAR SYMBOLISM IN CHINA

Apples symbolize peace.

Mandarins symbolize luck.

A sticky rice cake made for New Year's suggests that those who eat it will grow, in all senses of the word, for the new year.

Dumplings symbolize luck — this comes from their shape, which is similar to traditional gold ingots.

Pineapples symbolize wealth and prosperity.

Chicken symbolizes a good omen.

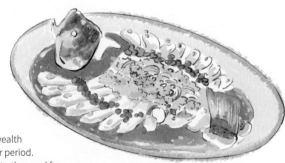

Fish, a symbol of prosperity, attracts wealth to a household for the whole New Year period. Its pronunciation in Mandarin is close to the word for "abundance." It is served whole (with the head) and only rarely is it all eaten. Not finishing the fish means that there will always be a surplus in the new year.

STREET FOOD

Street food in China is more than a simple culinary tradition: it is a culture unto itself. It goes back to the time of the Song dynasty (around the year 965 CE), when there were already night markets where people could eat on the go. Since then, this tradition has been handed down from father to son, from generation to generation, up to today.

You can eat at any time in China. Almost everywhere you go, you will find small stalls on wheels featuring simple cuisine where you can buy freshly prepared food, hot and steaming, that can be eaten in just a few bites. The streets of China are alive with street food.

Starting at 6 o'clock in the morning, as you stroll along the road, you can smell *youtiao* (fried doughnuts) and see the steam escaping from bamboo baskets in which *baozi* are cooked. A little farther on, people are busy kneading dough and stuffing won tons for their first customers. At noon, you can devour a stuffed *jianbing* (a Tianjin crepe), a Shaanxi *rou jia mo* (Chinese hamburger) or a dish of noodles made on site.

For a snack, you can share a *cong you bing* (green onion pancake) with friends if you feel like a savory food, or a red bean or black sesame soup if you have a sweet tooth.

As night falls, you can eat *malatang*, vegetables or meat on skewers to dip in a spicy broth, or barbecued meat skewers.

油条

冰糖葫芦

Youtiao: long savory doughtnuts made from wheat flour, with a crispy outside and a soft inside.

Bing tanghulu: skewers of different fruits coated with caramelized sugar. In the past, they were made with hawthorn berries, whose sour flesh contrasts with the sweet crunch of the coating.

葱油饼

米鸦水.

肉夹馍

Cong you bing: small pancakes made from wheat flour that are fried and garnished with green onions, a simple treat that everyone enjoys.

Sweet soup made from red beans

Rou jia mo: round bread with pork that has been cooked for a long time with spices and soy sauce; you can also add fresh cilantro and raw green chilies.

猪肠粉

鱼蛋粉

生煎包

Cheung fun (steamed rice noodle roll)

Rice noodles with fish balls

Shanghai grilled pork *bao*

碗仔翅

椰奶冻、

Imitation "shark fin" soup made from vermicelli and meat

Coconut jelly

SPRING ROLLS

Spring rolls are a very popular street food in China; people eat them for breakfast or for an afternoon snack. They can also be served at the table.

Thawing time: 2 hours to overnight
Preparation: 40 minutes
Cooking time: 20 minutes
Resting time: 10 minutes

MAKES 20 ROLLS

- ½ package spring roll wrappers
- 2 whole eggs + 1 yolk
- 1 tbsp. + 1 tbsp. (15 ml + 15 ml) vegetable oil
- ¼ lb. (120 g) garlic chives
- ½ lb. (250 g) soybean sprouts
- 1 tbsp. (15 ml) light soy sauce
- 1 tbsp. (15 ml) sesame oil
- Salt
- Neutral oil to fry the rolls

1 Thaw the spring roll wrappers for 2 hours at room temperature (you can also thaw the unopened package in the fridge overnight).

2 In a bowl, beat the whole eggs. Cook in a wok with 1 tablespoon of vegetable oil, breaking up the small clumps using a pair of chopsticks or a fork. Transfer to a plate.

3 Wash the chives and mince finely. Heat the rest of the oil in the wok, then stir fry the soybean sprouts until tender. Set aside on a plate.

4 Place the chives in the wok and stir fry for 1 minute. Add the soybean sprouts. Add the soy sauce, sesame oil and salt. Mix well. Let this stuffing cool for 10 minutes.

5 Place one thawed spring roll wrapper on the countertop, positioning one of the corners toward you. Place one heaping teaspoon of filling in the middle. Fold the lower corner toward the middle of the sheet, then the left corner and the right corner. Roll up. Brush a little beaten egg yolk on the top corner and close up the roll. Make the other rolls in the same way.

6 Heat the oil in a skillet over high heat, then brown the rolls for 2 to 3 minutes.

Stall selling *cong you bing*, pancakes garnished with green onions

FESTIVALS AND TRADITIONS

The lives of Chinese people are punctuated by traditional festivals that unfold throughout the lunar calendar. For each festival, there are age-old customs and traditions, which can vary from one region to another.

BIRTHDAYS AND WEDDINGS

In China, although birthdays are celebrated every year, special importance is given to those in the first year of life and certain years beginning at 60 (60, 66, 70, 80, 88, 90, 99...) — even numbers are preferred. These birthdays are celebrated with a festive meal and many gifts.

100 DAYS CELEBRATION

The 100 days celebration marks when a newborn passes the 100-day milestone. There are no strict rules about which dishes to serve: the aim is to choose dishes whose names evoke good omens, luck and happiness.

HAVING THE CHILD CHOOSING AN OBJECT ON THEIR FIRST BIRTHDAY

Before the birthday dinner is the *zhua zhou* ("grabbing one year") ritual.

A large platter containing different objects is placed on the floor in front of the baby, then the baby is allowed to choose (without any help) their favorite object. Depending on the object chosen, this can give an idea of their future: educated if they pick up a book, artist if it's a paintbrush, financier if they grab money or the abacus and so on.

The essential dish to celebrate this birthday is noodles, preferably very long, thin noodles, which are symbols of longevity. For the birthdays of older people, steamed buns in the shape of a peach, a symbol of longevity and vitality, are also served.

People do not celebrate the ages of 73 and 83 in China, as these were the ages when the philosphers Confucius and Mencius, respectively, died.

WEDDINGS IN CHINA

Although Chinese weddings are becoming more and more like Western ones, some ancient traditions are still in use today. Here are a few typical aspects of a Chinese wedding.

The color red plays an essential role in Chinese weddings, as it represents success, being joined together, loyalty, happiness, prosperity, love, fertility, etc. And so, the wedding decor is red, as is the bride's dress. The home and the room where the celebration takes place is decorated with the character "double happiness" in red, which is uniquely reserved for weddings.

Unlike in the Western tradition, the groom goes to pick up the bride at her home. The bride is kept in a room; a few of her friends (a little like bridesmaids) are in front of the door and ask questions of the groom, teasing him. The friends must be persuaded by the groom with red envelopes filled with money before they will hand over the bride. Then the couple bows to the bride's parents, offering them some tea that contains lotus seeds (a symbol of fertility) and jujube fruit (luck); if the parents accept the tea, that means they agree that their daughter can marry.

These four dried foods are commonly offered to the newly-weds: jujubes, peanuts, longans and lotus seeds, which symbolize the promise to have children soon.

103

LANTERN FESTIVAL

The Lantern Festival takes place on the 15th day of the first month of the lunar calendar in China. It is traditional to eat *yuan xiao* or *tang yuan* (rice dumplings with a sweet or savory filling). The round shape of the ball symbolizes unity in the family. Trying to solve the riddles written on the lanterns is a traditional and very popular activity. If you guess the answer to the riddle, you can win a gift.

TANG YUAN WITH BLACK SESAME SEEDS

MAKES 24 BALLS

For the filling
- 3 oz. (80 g) black sesame powder
- 2 tbsp. (30 ml) sugar
- 2 oz. (60 g) melted butter
- 1 pinch of salt

For the dough
- 3.4–3.7 oz. (100–110 ml) hot water
- 4 oz. (110 g) glutinous rice flour
- ⅓ oz. (10 g) rice flour

1 Combine all the filling ingredients, then refrigerate for at least 30 minutes.

2 Make the dough: In a bowl, combine the hot water with the two rice flours. Make a smooth and fairly soft ball. Cover with plastic wrap and let rest for 15 minutes at room temperature. Take 1 teaspoon of filling and roll it between your palms to make a ball. Make 24 balls in total. With the dough, make a thin sausage shape, then cut it into 24 pieces. Roll one piece between your palms to make a small ball. Flatten it with your fingers into a small disk. Place one little ball of filling in the middle of the disk. Bring the edges toward the center, enclosing the filling with the dough, then gently roll the ball between your palms. Do the same thing with the remaining balls.

3 Bring 6 cups (1.5 liters) of water to a boil in a large saucepan. Add the balls and stir gently. Cover and cook. When the balls come back to the surface, continue cooking for 1 to 2 minutes. Serve hot or warm with the cooking broth.

DRAGON BOAT FESTIVAL

This festival takes place on the fifth day of the fifth month of the lunar calendar. In southern China, the custom is to organize races of dragon-shaped boats to commemorate the famous poet Qu Yuan, from the Warring States period (around 475 to 221 BCE).

The signature food for this festival is *zong zi*. These are small rice dumplings, shaped like hard candies and wrapped in bamboo leaves. The fillings are quite varied, with, for example, marinated pork for a savory version and red bean puree for a sweet version.

MID-AUTUMN FESTIVAL/ MOON FESTIVAL

This festival, the second largest after Chinese New Year, takes place on the 15th day of the eighth month of the Chinese calendar, the day of the full moon. Because the shape of the full moon symbolizes harmonious gathering, this festival marks a precious time of family homecoming.

The Mid-Autumn Festival was originally an agricultural festival – the harvest celebration. Since the Tang Dynasty (618–907 CE), rites have been held in the imperial palace on this occasion.

In China, autumn is considered the finest season, rather dry and mild, and the mid-autumn moon is deemed to be the roundest and most beautiful. For these reasons, the festive activities are often held outdoors, under the moon, so people can contemplate it: a nocturnal picnic or a barbecue on the deck are very popular, and children wander around with lit lanterns. Farmers celebrate the harvest and the end of the growing season.

For this festival, people eat *yue bing*, or moon cakes. These cakes are in the shape of the full moon, which symbolizes gathering with family. The surface of these cakes is often decorated with patterns in relief with Chinese characters. They can be sweet or savory, and the fillings vary widely by region.

Cantonese *yue bing*

Other common foods for this festival:

Pomelo   Pomegranate   Osmanthus cake

CHINESE NEW YEAR

Chinese New Year is called the "Spring Festival" in China because it is considered the start of spring. This is the biggest festival in the country. The festivities happen over about 15 days and end with the Lantern Festival (see p. 104).

THE LEGEND

Once upon a time, there was a ferocious animal called Nian. Every year, it came down from the mountains on the eve of the New Year to attack the villages and devour the people. As the years passed, the villagers discovered his weaknesses: he was afraid of lights, noise and the color red. And so, every year, as the New Year drew near, people hung red decorations on their doors and windows, lit red lanterns and set off firecrackers to scare Nian away. This tradition continues today.

TRADITIONS AND CUSTOMS

The Little New Year: This is a celebration to say goodbye to the Kitchen (or Hearth) God. It takes place on the 23rd or 24th of the 12th lunar month. As they do each year, people ask for the family's good and/or bad actions to be taken to the Jade Emperor (ruler of the Heavens). For clemency, people place foods in front of his image, hoping to prevent him from saying bad things.

The house is cleaned from top to bottom, and old items are thrown away to drive out negative energies.

Red papers are stuck on the doors and windows, with words written on them, such as "happiness" or "spring." On each side of the front door, people attach a band of red paper on which a verse is written. The two verses respond to each other and form a parallel text.

People stock up on groceries as stores close for the holidays. New clothing is bought, especially for children.

New Year's Eve: The New Year's Eve meal is often held with the father's family. It is the biggest meal of the year and often includes symbolic dishes to ensure health, prosperity, luck, abundance and so on. These are some of the essential dishes: the word for fish (*yu*) is a homophone for "surplus." In the North, people eat *jiaozi* (dumplings), as their shape resembles that of ancient gold ingots; and *nian gao* (a sweet rice cake) because *gao* is a homophone for "high" — so eating it is a token of growth in all the desired areas.

Elders give cash in red envelopes to children and unmarried young people.

Firecrackers are lit around midnight to welcome the new year.

New Year's Day: People visit grandparents and elders, wear new clothes and, in some regions, eat a vegetarian meal. Visiting the temple is also a popular activity.

Day 2: Married women visit their families.

Day 5: People welcome Caishen, the God of Wealth.

PASTRIES AND DRINKS

Although dessert is not served after a meal in China, there is a very long list of sweets to be eaten throughout the day. Small crusty or soft cakes are perfect with a cup of tea or a tisane, and refreshing soups and crushed-ice smoothies are popular in summer.

MOON CAKES

During the Mid-Autumn Festival (see p. 106–107), people eat *yue bing* (moon cakes) with family members while admiring the full moon.

TYPES OF MOON CAKES

Sweet or savory, filled with candied fruit, legumes or meat, moon cakes vary from region to region.

广式月饼

Cantonese *yue bing*

潮月式酥饼

Chaozhou puff pastry *yue bing*

自来红

Peking *yue bing* with dried fruit

云南云腿月饼

Yunnan ham *yue bing*

蛋黄酥

Salted egg cakes

冰皮月饼

Snow skin *yue bing*

苏式月饼

Suzhou pork *yue bing*

SNOW SKIN YUE BING

Preparation: 1 hour
Resting time: 30 minutes
Cooking time: 15 minutes
Refrigeration: 2 hours

MAKES 12 CAKES

- Moon cake mold

For the filling

- 4 oz. (120 g) ground black sesame seeds
- ¾ oz. (20 g) melted butter
- 3 tbsp. (45 ml) liquid honey (acacia)

- 1 tbsp. (15 ml) partly skimmed milk
- Superfine sugar to taste

For the dough

- ⅓ cup (45 g) glutinous rice flour
- 1¼ oz. (35 g) rice flour
- ¾ oz. (20 g) wheat starch

- ¾ cup (177 ml) partly skimmed milk or soy milk
- 4 tsp. (20 ml) vegetable oil
- 2 to 3 tbsp. (24–36 g) superfine sugar
- Cornstarch for dusting

1 Make the filling: In a skillet, toast the sesame seeds in a dry pan for 5 minutes over medium heat, then process in a food processor. Place in a bowl. Add the melted butter and honey; stir. Add the milk and make a smooth ball. Add some sugar to taste. Set aside in the fridge.

2 Make the dough: In a bowl, combine all the ingredients until smooth. Let rest for 30 minutes at room temperature. Cook the dough in a heat-proof bowl in a steamer for 15 minutes. Remove dough from steamer and mix right away using a spatula to help cool it and ensure it's a smooth consistency. Allow it to cool.

3 With the cooled dough, make a thin sausage shape, then cut it into 12 equal pieces. Shape the dough into balls and then flatten them into small disks about ⅛ in. (3 mm) thick. Remove the filling from the fridge. Take one heaping teaspoon of filling, then roll it to make a ball. Place the filling in the center of a disk of dough. Prepare the other disks the same way.

4 Make a well with your left thumb and index finger. With your right hand, take one filled ball and place it in the well. Bring the edge of the disk toward the top of the well, pushing gently with the inside of your thumb to cover the ball of filling. Gently move the disk and repeat the steps until you can pinch it closed with your right index finger and thumb. Roll the ball in your hands until it is round and smooth.

5 Lightly dust one moon cake ball with cornstarch. Put the ball into the moon cake mold and press firmly for 30 seconds. Depending on the mold, you might be able to push the moon cake out of the mold or tap the mold on the countertop until the moon cake releases. Do the same for the other cakes. Refrigerate for 2 hours.

PEKING IMPERIAL CAKES

These cakes used to be for the major ceremonies of the imperial court. Later they were popularized.

枣花酥

Puff pastry cake with jujube puree filling

山楂锅盔

Cake with hawthorn puree filling

墨子酥

Cake with black sesame filling

状元饼

Cake with pork, salty egg yolk and mung bean filling

绿豆饼

Mung bean cake

黑芝麻椒盐

Black sesame and Sichuan pepper cake

牛舌饼

Ox-tongue shaped cake

豆沙饼

Cake with red bean filling

南瓜饼

Cake with pureed pumpkin filling

In southern China, you will find cakes often made with salted duck egg yolks, steamed cakes and Western-influenced tartlets.

STEAMED SPONGE CAKE

Resting time: 2 hours
Preparation: 15 minutes
Cooking time: 30 minutes

SERVES 4 OR 5

- 3 eggs at room temperature
- ½ cup (100 g) brown or muscovado sugar
- 1 cup (120 g) pastry flour
- 3½ tbsp. (50 ml) whole milk at room temperature

- ¼ cup (60 g) butter, melted
- 1 heaping tsp. (5 g) baking powder
- 1 tbsp. (15 ml) water

1 Beat the eggs with an electric mixer, then gradually add the sugar while beating for 5 to 6 minutes. The mixture should double or triple in volume and be very creamy. Gradually add the sifted flour, then the milk, and mix gently.

2 Let the mixture rest, covered with plastic wrap, for 1 to 2 hours at room temperature.

3 Melt the butter and add to the mixture. Dilute the baking powder in 2 teaspoons of water, add to the mixture and stir again gently.

4 Line a steamer basket or a 7-in. (18-cm) cake pan with parchment paper, add the dough and then the steamer cover. If you are using a cake pan, place the pan in large pot with a steam rack (trivet) and be sure to cover the lid with a tea towel so the condensation does not fall on the cake.

5 Let the mixture rest for a few minutes — the time needed to heat the cooking water. Fill a saucepan (the same diameter as the steamer basket) two-thirds full of water and bring to a boil. Place the steamer basket on the saucepan and cook for 30 minutes over high heat. At the end of the cooking time, wait 5 minutes before removing the lid so the cake doesn't sink. Serve hot or warm.

TANG SHUI AND BAOBING

In China, there is there is a category of sweet dishes in the form of soups (hot or cold) or custards whose generic name is *tang shui* or *tong sui* in Cantonese. They are delicately sweetened and low in calories. Their sweetness is comforting.

红豆沙

Simmered sweet soup with red beans

芝麻糊

Black sesame soup

杨枝甘露

Mango and pomelo smoothie with tapioca pearls

豆腐花

Silky tofu with sweet topping

GINGER MILK PUDDING

Preparation: 15 minutes
Cooking time: 2 minutes
Resting time: 10 minutes

SERVES 4

- 4 oz. (120 g) ginger
- 2½ cups (600 ml) whole milk
- ½ cup (40–60 g) icing sugar

姜撞奶

1 Peel the ginger, grate it into a puree, then squeeze, using clean cheese cloth, to get the juice. Mix the juice well and divide into four small bowls. This will make about 4 tablespoons (60 ml) of pressed ginger juice.

2 Place the milk in a saucepan, add the sugar and heat to 176–185°F (80–85°C), stirring often to dissolve the sugar.

3 Remove from heat and let cool to 158–167°F (70–75°C).

4 Pour ⅝ cup (150 ml) of milk over the ginger juice in the first bowl, keeping each bowl 4 in. (10 cm) apart, then do the same for the other three bowls.

5 Let rest 7 to 10 minutes. Do not stir and do not move the bowls during the resting time.

Baobing is a great summer dessert. There are countless varieties. Start by finely shaving ice, then drizzling the ice with a form of liquid sugar (honey, syrup, condensed milk, custard, and so on) and adding pieces of fresh or dried fruit, mochi balls, tapioca, red beans and so on.

CAKES MADE FROM RICE

Sweet, soft and melt-in-your-mouth, sticky rice pairs perfectly with sweet ingredients. These cakes are often eaten hot, warm or at room temperature but rarely cold or frozen.

驴打滚

Lüdagun (literally, "donkeys rolling on the ground") is a rolled cake with red bean filling that is coated in toasted soy flour.

青团

Qing tuan is a dumpling made from glutinous rice flour and mugwort leaves.

麻球

Matuan is a pastry made of rice flour that has been fried and covered in sesame seeds.

糯米枣

Jujubes stuffed with rice-flour cake

年糕

Nian gao is a sticky rice cake made for the New Year.

汤圆

Tang'yuan consists of stuffed rice dumplings served in broth or syrup.

EIGHT TREASURE RICE CAKE

SERVES 3 OR 4

- 5 oz. (150 g) short-grain rice
- ¾ oz. (20 g) jujube fruit
- ½ oz . (15 g) dried longans
- ⅓ oz. (10 g) lotus seeds
- ⅓ oz. (10 g) peanuts
- ⅓ oz. (10 g) walnut kernels
- 1 tbsp. (5 g) Goji berries
- ⅓ oz. (10 g) raisins
- 2–2½ oz. (50–70 g) sweet red bean paste
- A little oil for the bowl

1 The night before, rinse the rice then soak overnight.

2 Cook the rice in an electric rice cooker or in a pot.

3 Remove the stones from the jujubes if they are whole. Place for 1 minute in boiling water to remove the bitterness. Drain and dry with paper towel.

4 Oil a heat-proof flat-bottomed bowl. Cut all the dried fruit except the Goji berries and raisins into pieces and spread all the dried fruit in the bottom of the bowl.

5 Cover the dried fruit with half the rice, then spread the red bean paste over the rice. Next spread the other half of the rice on top. Press down well so the mixture is compact.

6 Steam for 10 minutes in a steamer. Turn the bowl upside down on a plate to unmold.

CHINESE TEAS

Tea is thought to have have originated in southwestern China. Its use as a drink dates from prehistoric times. It has a central place in the lives of Chinese people, who drink tea from morning to night, at home and at work, at restaurants with a meal or from a thermos so they can quench their thirst wherever they go.

Chinese teas are classified by the color of their leaves when they are used: there are green, yellow, white, red, black and oolong teas. So, how are these different colors of teas determined? Tea leaves, like all plants, contain oxidizing enzymes that are responsible for the yellowing of the leaves. Once the leaves are picked, oxidation of the pigments and tannins that they contain begins. This phenomenon of oxidation determines the color of the tea. Teas that are less oxidized make up green tea, white tea and yellow tea. The darker the color of the leaves, the more oxidized the teas are.

THE BEST-KNOWN TEAS IN CHINA

Longjing ("dragon well") green tea has an umami-rich and very refreshing flavor.

Huangshan ("yellow mountain") *mao feng* green tea has a gentle, delicate flavor.

Rock oolong tea is full-bodied and smoky with a long finish in the mouth.

Red teas are ideal for cold and damp weather.

Tie guan yin oolong tea is rich and complex in the nose and on the palate.

Pu-erh is a lively tea that can get better over time thanks to the fermentation process.

GONG FU CHA

This is a Chinese method of making tea, a congenial way of appreciating a good tea (a little like oenologists preparing us for a wine tasting). A good amount of leaves is used, and they are infused in small 5-ounce (150-ml) teapots; this gives a rich and strong infusion but with no bitterness. The infused tea is served in very small cups, and each cup is often drunk all at once.

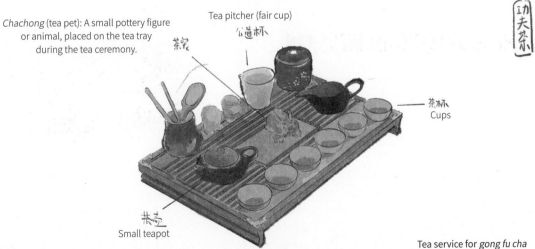

Chachong (tea pet): A small pottery figure or animal, placed on the tea tray during the tea ceremony.

Tea pitcher (fair cup)

Cups

Small teapot

Tea service for *gong fu cha*

DRINKS WITH HEALTH BENEFITS

In China, people like hot drinks. In addition to tea, there are many infusions made from flowers, herbs, dried fruit, roots and so on. These infusions are called *yang sheng cha*: tea to nourish life. People choose the appropriate infusion based on the state of their health and the micro-seasons.

Here are some classic infusions:

Liang cha: broth made of medicinal herbs such as mulberry leaves, honeysuckle, licorice, etc.

Suan mei tang: infusion made of black plums, licorice, dried clementine peel and hawthorn.

JUJUBE AND LONGAN INFUSION

- 4 cups (1 l) spring water
- 8–10 dried jujube fruits
- 6 dried longans
- A dozen Goji berries
- Brown sugar to taste

1 Cut each jujube in half lengthwise. Remove the stone. Remove the skin from the longans.

2 In a saucepan, add the water, jujubes and longans, bring to a boil, then simmer 10 minutes over low heat. Add the Goji berries and steep 15 to 20 minutes. Add sugar to taste. Serve hot or warm.

GINGER AND BLACK SUGAR TISANE

I often make this tisane, which is well known for its ability to fight colds and temporary fatigue during cold spells. According to Chinese medicine, black sugar is good for warming up the stomach and stimulating blood circulation.

- 3⅓ cup (800 ml) spring water or filtered water
- 3-in. piece ginger (with skin), cut in thin slices
- ½–1 oz. (15–30 g) black sugar

1 Add the water to a saucepan, then add the ginger.

2 Bring to a boil, then reduce heat and simmer for 20 to 30 minutes.

3 Add the black sugar at the end of cooking, stir well and serve.

I never peel the ginger, as the skin adds flavor and, above all, maintains the nutritional balance of the ginger: the skin is the *yin* and the flesh is the *yang*. According to Chinese medicine, if there is only *yang*, this creates an imbalance, which means excess energy!

CHRYSANTHEMUM AND GOJI BERRY TISANE

This tisane made from chrysanthemums and Goji berries is known for brightening the eyes, protecting vision and nourishing the liver.

- 4 cups (1 l) spring water
- 1 tbsp. (7 g) Goji berries
- 1 tbsp. (3 g) dried chrysanthemum flowers

1 Bring 4 cups (1 liter) of spring water to a simmer.

2 Steep the Goji berries and chrysanthemum flowers in the water for 5 to 10 minutes. Serve.

ALCOHOL

In the distant past, a man named Du Kang lived along the Yellow River. One day,
he decided to leave the leftover grains of his meal in the trunk of a dead tree.
A few days later, a pleasant odor wafted from the tree, and a liquid flowed
from it. Du Kang put a drop in his mouth and was pleasantly surprised.
That is how alcohol came to be, according to the legend.

选料
Choosing the grain

蒸馏
Steaming the grain

制曲
Making the yeast

发酵
Fermentation

勾兑
Stirring before bottling

陈酿
Aging

The rotten grains (rice, sorghum, millet, wheat, etc.) were later named *jiuqu* by Chinese people. These are
the most common yeasts for making traditional alcohols in China.

SHAOXING ALCOHOL

Also called "Shaoxing wine," this is one of the most popular alcohols in China. It is often drunk warm after being steeped with dried salted plums for at least 30 minutes.

SHAOXING WINE WITH SALTED PLUMS

1 Combine the wine and the plums in a carafe. Add one salted plum per each cup of wine.

2 Heat the carafe in a double boiler to 122–140°F (50-60°C). Steep the plums for at least 30 minutes.

3 Drink warm.

> You can use lower-quality Shaoxing wine for cooking.

BAIJIU, DISTILLED CLEAR ALCOHOL

This alcohol is distilled from traditional grains. It is made from fermented sorghum and often mixed with wheat, corn, millet or Tibetan barley.

In China, *baijiu* is usually drunk as a shot, all at once, and people say "*Ganbei*" ("dry cup") when they toast. It is almost custom to drink *baijiu* at events such as weddings or birthdays and also at a meal to complete a major contract between two businesses.

Mild premixed cocktails are sold in cans. They are very popular with the younger generations.

INDEX

RECIPE INDEX

MARGOT'S ACKNOWLEDGMENTS

I wish to sincerely thank Aurélie, my editor, for having confidence in me through all these years. Heartfelt thanks to my illustrator, Zhao En, for his wonderful work, which gave our project soul and plenty of charm.

Krys, without you I wouldn't have met Zhao En, and all this would not have been possible.

And finally, a loving thank you to my husband and a thought for my son, Paul, in the hopes that he will love Chinese cuisine even more upon reading this book.

ZHAO EN YANG'S ACKNOWLEDGMENTS

感谢张老师以及法国Mango出版社的编辑Aurélie的信任与等待，感谢笔墨文化的Jia'yi帮忙翻译以及协调，让我有足够的时间空间去完成。感恩一切，愿你们能在这些中国美食里感受到温度以及热情，还有那些隐藏在食物里的爱。

I would like to thank the author, Margot, and Aurélie at Mango Publishing for their trust and patience; thank you also to Jiayi at BiMot Culture for translation and coordination. Thanks to you, I had enough time and space to complete this project. Thank you for everything. I hope you can experience warmth and passion while discovering Chinese cooking, and that in food you will find love.

A FIREFLY BOOK

Published by Firefly Books Ltd. 2024
First published in French by Mango, Paris, France – 2023
© Mango, Paris, 2023
Translation © Firefly Books Ltd. 2024
Text and recipes © Margot Zhang
Illustrations © Zhao En Yang

Translated by Anne Louise Mahoney

First printing

Published in Canada by
Firefly Books Ltd.
50 Staples Avenue, Unit 1
Richmond Hill, Ontario
L4B 0A7

Published in the United States by
Firefly Books (U.S.) Inc.
P.O. Box 1338, Ellicott Station
Buffalo, New York
14205

Printed in China | E

Library of Congress Control Number: 2024935704

Library and Archives Canada Cataloguing in Publication
Title: Chinese cuisine : recipes and anecdotes from Chinese gastronomic culture / written by Margot Zhang ; illustrated by Zhao En Yang.
Other titles: Cuisine chinoise illustrée. English
Names: Zhang, Margot, author. | Yang, Zhao En, illustrator.
Description: Includes index. | Translation of: La cuisine chinoise illustrée.
Identifiers: Canadiana 20240356225 | ISBN 9780228105152 (softcover)
Subjects: LCSH: Cooking, Chinese. | LCSH: Gastronomy—China. | LCSH: Cooking, Chinese—Pictorial works. | LCSH: Gastronomy—China—Pictorial works. | LCSH: Cooking, Chinese—Anecdotes. | LCSH: Gastronomy—China—Anecdotes. | LCGFT: Cookbooks. | LCGFT: Illustrated works. | LCGFT: Anecdotes.
Classification: LCC TX724.5.C5 Z5313 2024 | DDC 641.5951—dc23

Canadä

We acknowledge the financial support of the Government of Canada.